Trauma Has No Color

T BALFOUR

CHERI LEE FLEMING

ANDREA FOREMAN

AMANDA GRANT

JADA HARPER

LAJUAN HAWKINS

OLIVIA JANOCHA

JAS

BRANDY POOLE-LEE

UMUNIQUE NEVAHA

ASHLEY PAINTER

AMBER GRAVER-ROOF

SARA

LOGAN WASIUTA

LOGOS

COMMUNITY DEVELOPMENT
CORPORATION

M000315560

ISBN: 978-0-578-97059-2

Published by Logos CDC

www.logoscdc.org

Harrington, Delaware

Printed in the United States of America

Contents

I Am Not My Trauma

Ashley Painter

As I sit here tearing up writing this, the very thought of having to uncover these thoughts makes me emotional. I am not in a place where I can completely disclose all the details of what I endured.

Before my trauma, I enjoyed getting my hair and nails done, going out to eat with friends and family. I loved the beach and would go even if I went alone. I enjoyed going out and doing anything. I enjoyed life and everything it had to offer. I always wanted to make memories, have lots of friends, and enjoy my loving family. I was a girl who loved her dad, did everything with him, and could tell him anything. My sister was my heart and the world to me; I prayed for her. I was walking the red road the best I could. I loved endlessly, cared too much. I struggled in my relationship with my mom. I stood my ground in my beliefs and took nothing from no one.

My trauma has changed me tremendously. I can't just snap my fingers and go back to the person I used to be. I lost so much. I lost my sense of safety and security, trust and innocence. I also lost friends that I will never get back or reconnect with again. I lost my ability to see the good in people, always believing that there were ulterior motives.

A monster snuck up behind me, and I never saw it coming. I was clothed like a sheep, so beautiful and sweet. Underneath was something so deranged and dangerous that engulfed me before I realized that I was being swallowed. I lost my freedom and lived life in chains. I painted the picture of the chains not being in existence but knowing that they were. My identity was ripped away from me, and I lost my total embodiment of self. I questioned who I was and why I was still here. My trauma left me with invisible scars and nightmares that are never-ending.

My trauma has changed me; it has left me with invisible scars and nightmares that never end. Out of misery and pain came strength and power. It takes strength to stay in a situation that you know could possibly end your life. It takes strength to stay when you know that each day could be your last. It takes even more strength to leave, sever all ties, and to stay gone.

I am not my trauma, for that was something that I conquered. I am not a victim, but I was victimized. Out of victimization rose a strong, powerful intelligent, woman.

Dear Ash,

I hope you know that when he begins yelling on Christmas night, you are okay, and Toby will be too. Get your things together and run. I promise you will be okay. Make sure to wake mom and dad and tell JR sooner. Know this is what is best for you. Talk to mom and let dad go nuts on him. All this will make you better and move home. Remember, this is temporary, and you are stronger. I was in your corner rooting for you. Sometimes people go through tough times. This time was hard because I had never allowed or had someone do the things he did. He downgraded the way I was raised. He objected and criticized me for wearing makeup. Yes, you are strong, but he was stronger. It is ok and normal to feel scared, unsure, alone, like you let dad down, and like you are not enough. Sometimes you are just too hard on yourself. I know you will get through because you are brave. You are strong, you are your father's child, and you are a warrior. The most valuable piece of advice I am going to give you is to talk more with mom. She loves you and will always love you and has your back and absolutely will help you.

Yours truly,

Ash

CHAPTER TWO

Met·a·mor·pho·sis

Brandy Poole-Lee

Do you believe that a rose can grow from concrete? If you do not, believe me, I grew.

They say your first love is your mother. Once in my life, I believed in that fairytale as a child. The older I became, the dream faded away. Have you ever felt like you were enough for her? You know, like her light in her darkness, a sunbeam on a gloomy day. If you are, cool, great for you. Great for you! Look at you having a great mom. I am happy for you, honestly. But where are the people who grew up with a broken mother? Where are the people that grew up surrounded by old demons, waiting, lurking to strike them down any at every corner? Those demons were ready to destroy any bliss of my happiness.

If this is you, congratulations, friend; you are part of the "Broken Mothers Club." It's an elite group. Some will survive, and others will thrive from the ash from their mother's sowing; well, at least I did. The last time I heard my mom tell me that she loved me was 20 years ago when we moved to Dover, Delaware. I was re-rooted from a place called home. I was surrounded by love, care and watered by family. Just to be moved 203 miles away caused my mother's love to be lost. "Brandy, we moved here for a job opportunity!" This meant "your father once again made a fool out of me, and I can't bear the pain of what has become of me." She was always running from her problems that ended up being my life. I know she was praying to God that the problem would go away. As a child, I never understood how two people who used to love each other could hurt each other. They did not know those actions made another human grow up feeling unwanted.

Living on 19 Starboard Court felt like a UFC fight. I was blocking, dodging comments, slight looks, and unspoken words that still hold unforgiven pain. I felt like I could not do anything right in her eyes. As a preteen, I saw what depression looked and felt like. It was dark and cold as if it was a morgue. You could hear every step and creak that settled. The neighbors were speaking in their native tongue. I felt alone; I grew alone; I was alone. My mother was a fighter ready for a win. I was always saying sorry and battled feelings of shame for the arguments she caused. She was a narcissist!

She knew what button to push and what storyline to play. "Do you see how this makes me feel, Brandy?" "What? That didn't happen; this is what happened!" See, now that is a lie! What type of mother do you want? It is not tit for tat! What I am saying is ...Mom, it is a tit for tat, knowing mother has the trauma that she did not overcome. My mother never knew that I was experiencing abuse as a child, just like her. My innocence was compromised just like hers. I am being bullied at school, just to come home to go against the biggest bully of them all. Knowing as a child, I was going to lose, but I never gave up. I even fell into depression.

I remember my room became a dark, scary place. I could feel my soul leaving my body and someone stepping in. The walls closed in on me. I lost a lot of sleep. I remember having a bible next to me, and the same chapter continued to surface. It was over for me. Like this is it. I heard voices. My body felt cold. I was ready to go. I felt unloved and unwanted. What was my purpose in this life? I remembered praying to God, asking him to show me the way through this dark time in my life. If you do not believe that God is real, believe it! I had a relationship with him. There were times that I did not think he was listening to me. I still knew that he was real. Mother always told me I could count on him, but it was hard.

I was in an abusive relationship for about a year. I was at my end, and I was lost in love. I took many punches okay, insults, objects being thrown. I felt like no one loved me. I used to think, "Why am I here?" "Why does he do these awful things to me?" "Today is a great day to jump out of a three-story window." But I did not. He called the cops. I remember sitting on the concrete ground in North Carolina, asking Wake County Police to shoot me. I was mad, begging and bartering for them to take my life. I finally left him, and he tried to come back into my life after destroying it. After I no longer needed him, I went back to that same apartment.

I had this dream, and I told myself if I did not get out now, I would never get out. I called my best friend back at home and asked her to send me an Uber from his apartment to go back to campus. My boyfriend became so angry. He began to scream and yell at me. He said I owed him money. I remember trying to tune out the yelling and packing my things. I was not trying to deal with this guy wanting drama. I wanted to go home. Things began to escalate. His apartment was on the third floor. He started to push me and would not stop. He kept saying that I was trespassing and that he would call the police on me. He did not care that I was falling down the steps. He just kept on pushing me. I remember thinking that he was going to kill me. I felt like I was going to bust my head open.

A woman heard me screaming, and she ran toward me. She saved my life. She asked if I went to Shaw University. I told her that I was a student at that school. She fought the guy off for me then took me back to school. She told him that he was not going to do anything else to me. She told him that I was leaving and not to come anywhere near her car. She went Ham on him. I got into her car, and she took me back to campus. She said she was sent to that apartment that day to save me from the mess I was in. She also said that I should use that experience as a warning never to allow something like that to happen again.

My mother was heartbroken when I told her what happened to me. She had a similar experience and could empathize with my situation. My mother did not want me to go through the same thing that she had gone through.

That is why I knew my mom was not cold-hearted. I could see that she was a person. Knowing that my mother went through some of the same things I experienced helped me understand her better. She made me the powerful woman that I am today even though sometimes I feel like a hopeless child, looking for love in the wrong places. We are just two caterpillars ready for metamorphosis.

Met•a•mor•pho•sis /mədəmôrfəsəs/- The process of transformation from an immature form to an adult form in two or more distinct stages.

There are four stages of a butterfly. The egg represents a fresh new start. This is where innocence begins. Larva represents the youth living and learning. They are finding their way and will make mistakes. This phase also includes eating and absorbing things. The third stage is the pupa. This is the stage where the transition takes place. It may look like nothing is going on, but significant changes are happening inside. Special cells that were present in the larva are now growing rapidly. They will become the legs, wings, eyes, and other parts of the adult butterfly. Many of the original larva cells will provide energy for these growing adult cells.

The relationship between my mother and me is like the stages of a butterfly. We are just two beautiful creations soaring through a beautiful madness, ready to become one. As I sit here thinking with my pen flowing on the paper, I realize that the things that are flowing from my thoughts have never been shared with my mother. I know when I was a child, she was very overprotective of me. I never knew that her fears were embedded in the things she battled with as a child into her adulthood.

I am writing this chapter because I want everyone to know how I came to cherish life. I want my mother to know that I forgive her. I love my mother to the moon and back. I love my mother to the next galaxy. I know she is still trying to heal the wounds that seem to never close. I need my mother to know that I am here with her every step of the way. No matter how hard or angry I get, I want her to know that I am listening and taking every step she tells me to take. Maybe not all of them, but I am taking some. I now realize the things my mother said were not to hurt me but to protect and grow me. My mother is the best mom I could have ever asked for. I know that our relationship is not the best, but I believe it will get better.

Dear Brandy,

Baby girl, you are going to go through some fire. Yeah, it is going to hurt, but you will grow and fly to be a phoenix. You will become the person you always wanted to be. You might feel like giving up, but you cannot and will not because you're stronger than you see yourself in the mirror. You will bear a child, and he needs you more than anything. Be his first love. Explain to him what a man should be like. You will become everything you want to be. Your love will knock you down and spit you right back out and make a fool out of you. Just know you are not a fool. You are a fighter ready to battle in any Goliath. Ready, PUSH any barriers and walls.

You are not weak. You are strong; you do not need to beg anybody to stay who did not want to. You do not need to submit to anybody who is not ready to submit to you. Do not allow people to walk over you. Stand up for yourself. People will know your name and understand that you are a force to be reckoned with. You were raised and made from clay from a strong woman. This woman was raised from the ashes.

Failed relationships will not overtake you. You are stronger than you think. It is time to wake up and smell the roses. Pick yourself up! You are a goddess who knows what she stands for and what she does not stand for. You are a lover, a mother, a true believer, and a hard worker. Brandy, you are loveable, and you will find someone that will cherish you. Lastly, remember who the f*** you are, and that Mary had a little lamb.

CHAPTER THREE

The Birth Of Evolution

T. Balfour

We, as humans, like to think that we have control over our own lives. We think whatever we have in our plans can only go that way and will, but we do not have that complete control. There is no way to be prepared for trauma. Although, we hear about it and know we would be upset, hurt, and angry. That real emotion cannot exist until we as individuals have been put through that said trauma. To look at me, you would probably think I had a perfect life because I always had nice quality things. I was always smiling like I did not have a care in the world. I have been through a lot. I have carried so much on me the past 20 years of my life, and I am only 25. The first time I said those numbers out loud in the same sentence like that, it blew my mind. How is that even possible? I have not even lived yet! It most certainly is possible, and I am here today to let you into my life before the growth of self-love and care when things seemed so sweet but were not.

At just about four years old or so, I remember being at my aunt's house and being in the boys' bedroom. They were about eleven and twelve at the time. I sat on the bed by the youngest cousin while the older one sat on his bed on the other side of the room. They started talking amongst themselves about something, but I could not make out what they were saying. Then the youngest said, "Okay, I'm going to go first." He told me to lie back on the bed and then proceeded to cover us with his bright orange blanket. He then hovered over the top of me while he unzipped his pants and did his business. I can remember just seeing him, staring at him, and me moving up and down with his black do-rag and oversized t-shirt on. I did not recall experiencing any pain, so I did not feel the need to say anything about what had just happened. That was the first of many times that my youngest cousin had raped me.

The oldest at that time did not do anything afterward. They just told me that I could go back out of the room and play; that is just what I did. The second time I remember being at my aunt's house again, and I had to pee. When I knocked on the bathroom door, my youngest cousin had opened the door to let me in. I had a little potty in the bathroom as well, so I just used that while he was sitting completely naked on the toilet in front of me. When I was finished using the potty, I was about to pull my pants up when he said to me, "Come here and give me a hug." At that same time, he was pulling me towards him and then turned me away from him. I remember him picking me up and putting me on his lap, that being the next time he raped me. Again, I did not recall pain, so again I said nothing.

The third time being raped in total is when my oldest cousin finally decided to take his turn. The last time at my aunt's house, we were alone in his bedroom. His mattress was on the floor in front of the closet. He told me to lie down. I had on a white kid-size t-shirt and flowers on my undies. He was shirtless with just a pair of oversized jeans and boxers on. He took my undies off and hovered over me while he unzipped his pants to rape me. After he was finished, we heard my grandmother arriving for a visit. He frantically told me to put my undies on and not to say anything.

By now, you would think that I would have said something anyway to someone, but no, I did not. We went out into the living room where my grandmother and aunt were sitting and chatting. I hugged my grandmother and remembered her smile turning into concern. She had said, "Why are your panties inside out?" At that age, I was more than capable of putting my undies on properly. Before I could say anything at all, my oldest cousin blurted out, "She just came from the bathroom, that's all." My grandmother looked at me funny for a moment but let it go as I was not acting out of the ordinary. That was the first of two times that my oldest cousin raped me or even attempted.

The fourth time I was maybe about five. I was at my aunt's house. She was living with my cousins in Laurel behind a motel near Marino's car dealership. It was my first time staying there with them. The house was small. It only had one bedroom, a little bathroom, kitchen, and living room. It was nighttime, and I was up with my oldest cousin watching TV. My youngest cousin was sleeping on the floor in front of the television, and my aunt was asleep in the bedroom. I laid down with my oldest cousin on the couch, and I started to feel something poking me in the back. I looked down under the cover and saw that his penis was out. He quickly tried to cover himself, but I had already seen him exposed. I jumped up off the couch and ran into my aunt's room with her. She was a heavy sleeper. She did not notice me hiding behind her legs and watching to see if my oldest cousin was going to appear in the doorway. I said nothing.

The fifth and final time of being raped was at my great grandmother's at Savannah East apartments. My great-grandmother had gone to bed for the night, so my youngest cousin and I were the only ones awake. We were watching TV. I was lying on the day bed, and he was on the couch along the other wall. He had told me to come over to him, so I did. He told me to lie down on the couch. When I complied, he had hovered over me and raped me. He was wearing a black do-rag, a gray shirt with the sleeves cut off, and black basketball shorts. I had on a beater and basketball shorts. Again, I felt no pain but remember him going up and down again and staring at me just as he had the first time he raped me. After some time, he had stopped and told us to switch positions. He laid down on the couch, and I was sitting on the other end of the couch. He had his penis out and told me to put it in my mouth. I did. He told me to pretend like I was sucking a popsicle. At one point, he said, "Watch your teeth." He praised me when I got it right. He said, "Yeah, like that." After I was finished, I went to lay back down on the day bed and just laid there until I fell asleep because I did not feel right, but unfortunately again, I said absolutely nothing.

The first time I came out about the rape, I was about thirteen or fourteen and was "dating" some boy I had met in middle school. When I had told him, he said, "Ew. That's gross," as if I had told him, I was willingly having sex at the age of 4 with my eleven and twelve-year-old cousins. I was so shocked because I thought he cared about me, but I realized he did not. When I was about seventeen, I told my female cousin who happens to be the oldest sibling of my two cousins,. She was ready to take me down to the police station so that I could do a report. I did not want to go because I had not even told my mom this information yet. I did not know how to tell her. I knew she would be upset. I did not want her to risk her job at the Department of Corrections. I did not feel like I had a huge burden on me, but in reality, I did.

Shortly after, I told my grandmother. She was shocked and recalled the third time she asked me about my panties being on inside out. I confirmed the moment, and we sat in silence for a moment. She apologized because she should have done something then, but I told her it was okay. I also did not say anything to make her alarmed and feel the need to do anything. She said that she would not tell my mom and let me do it on my own.

When I was eighteen, I finally got enough guts to approach my mom about this and have a conversation. We met up at the Royal Farms. She had just gotten off work at the prison. She reacted in a way that I had not imagined. I thought she would explode and want to find my cousins. She immediately called the police department and had me report it. She said that she wished I had told her I was pregnant instead. At that moment, I knew my mom was going to blame herself. She thought, if she had not been working so much to take care of me and the household, I would not have been in those situations. I reassured her that she is a great mother, and it was not her fault. We both thought I was safe with the family.

I did my report and talked to an investigator, but since the incidences had occurred years ago and I had no physical evidence, there would not be any arrests. I assured the two ladies at the police station that I did not expect anything to be done about the rapes. I knew that a lot of time had passed since it happened. I wanted my mom to understand what had happened in my life. If I were a mother, I would hope that my children could come to me if something like this happened to them. I would want my children to be brave enough to speak up regardless of how they thought I would take it.

I found out that my youngest cousin was in jail down in Florida for raping his then stepdaughter at the time. He had started raping her when she was an infant, and it carried on for years. The final day was after she was found in the coat closet. He left her in the closet after he woke her up early before everyone got up for church. I carried guilt for some time. I had realized that I was raped. It was not a good thing at all; it was too late. He had gotten another innocent victim. If I had said something a lot sooner, just maybe she could have been saved. I had to learn that I was not thinking rationally and that there was no way I had control over that.

My next trauma was my biggest fear come true. July 17, 2020. My grandmother had called me to inform me that she could not get ahold of my oldest aunt. My aunt had some serious health problems over the years. She had Type 1 Diabetes resulting in her losing her eyesight, and half of her foot was amputated. She had multiple heart surgeries ranging from a triple bypass, open-heart surgery, stints put into valves, and a pacemaker placed in her chest. I had not thought anything of it because I just thought maybe she went to the bathroom and was not near her phone.

My grandmother missed the call from my aunt due to her being on another call. She did not get to call her back because she was getting herself together to do a double at work. I informed her that I would call and see if she picked up and that she should finish getting ready for work. I called a couple of times, but she never picked up. I had just gotten some steamed crabs to eat, so I was starting to crack open the first one. I got this feeling that resonated in my gut like I needed to put the food down and go to my aunt's house. My aunt lived in Milton, Delaware. I was living in Ellendale at the time with my then long-term boyfriend. It was not a feeling of anxiety or nervousness. I put the food away instantly. I told my boyfriend that I needed to check on my aunt and make sure she was okay. He said, "Okay," and stayed behind.

As I finally pulled into my aunt's driveway, I could see that her front door was wide open, but her screen door was closed. That was not something I ever knew my aunt to do. Her door was always closed. So, before I got out of the car, I called my mom and let her know something did not seem right. I walked up to the door and looked inside to see if I could see my aunt in the living room or kitchen. I saw only the dogs in their pen. I could also hear my aunt's phone ringing with her favorite song, "Take Me to the King" by Tamela Mann. Then I saw something move behind my aunt's power chair; it was her foot. I could then see my aunt lying on the floor face down, trying to move around and, I assume, get herself up off the floor. There was nothing around for her to grab hold of. I was not thinking. I just wanted to bust through the door. I said to my mom, "Oh my god, she's on the floor, and I can't get in because the screen door is locked! What do I do, Mom!" She told me to stay calm and dial 911.

I was frantic at this point. It took everything in me to stay calm and make the call beginning to end without breaking down. I just wanted my aunt to be okay, and I did not know what state she was in. When the operator asked me questions, I tried yelling into my aunt from the screen door because the glass part was up enough to talk to her. She was not responding to me. She was slurring her words, and at that point, she was mostly telling the dog to stop barking and that she could not find her phone. The ambulance arrived, and we were able to get the door opened without any damage. The EMTs started asking me questions regarding my aunt, such as name, birthdate, health conditions. Before I could say anything, my aunt had given all the information herself, even in the state that she was in. Shortly after, the EMTs took my aunt out on a stretcher to the ambulance.

After about two minutes, one of the EMTs came out to me and asked if my aunt usually talks if one side of her face is drooping down to one side. I replied no; then my heart started pounding because I already knew what they were going to say at that point. They allowed me to get into the ambulance to confirm how she looked. One of the EMTs rubbed my aunt's left leg and asked if she could feel it, "No," she replied. Then he rubbed her left arm and hand and asked if she could feel that, again she replied, "No." Then he said, "We're going to have to call it. We need to get her to the stroke center." The EMT finally asked my aunt if she knew who was with her at that moment. She replied, "I'm not sure, but probably my niece Tori." I could see her face, and it broke my heart because there was nothing I could do for her.

Over the course of the next few days of her stay at Bay health, she was doing rehab therapy to get feeling back into her left arm and leg, which happened. I was sure that she would be released soon and back home. Then one day, my family and I got updated that my aunt had a blood clot in her heart. Her heart was only working at 20% since her two heart attacks back in March of 2020. With her having diabetes, it would have been dangerous for the doctors to give her dye to see the exact location of the clot. We had to either see what happened or give her the dye. We waited to see what would happen.

August 1, 2020, at 3:26 AM, my mom called me and told me that I should get my then-boyfriend to drive me to the hospital because my aunt's heart had stopped. They did CPR on her for about 20 minutes and brought her back. I was unsure of how long she would stay with us. I dropped my phone and burst into tears, screaming as loud as I could as if that were going to bring her back. When I arrived at the hospital, my mom and grandmother were already there. They had already been to the back to see my aunt. My mom walked with me and held my hand as we took the long walk down the hallway to my aunt's room. The closer we got to her room, the weaker I started to feel. When we got to her door and saw her lifeless body, I had to catch myself. I went over to her bedside and just looked at her. She looked so peaceful. I began to burst into tears and tell her that I was sorry that I could not come to visit her in the hospital while she was alive. I was also supposed to do my first video chat with her that morning since she had been in the hospital.

I felt so numb and wished that I could have done more to keep her alive. I wished that I had just busted that screen door down and held her and told her I loved her until the ambulance came. My family told me to be proud of myself. If I had not listened to that gut feeling and checked on my aunt when I did, she could have died right there that day in her home.

I know death is a part of life that we cannot stop. It hurts like hell when someone you love is snatched away from you. It feels like you are being punched in the gut and face at the same time. I could not focus. I stopped eating for days at a time. I was not prepared to plan a funeral for my aunt who was only 53. She was a true angel and child of God. If it were not for her, I would not have gotten saved. I thanked her for never giving up on me and for praying over me as much as she did. She is also the reason for my nickname Bird, and I could not be more thankful for that either.

For about a month, I kept seeing her on the floor repeatedly, and I just wanted it to stop. I was in a mental place I never could have imagined. I hated it. But that was still nothing compared to how much deeper into a darkness I was about to go. August 16, 2020, just seven days after burying my aunt, my mom sent a group text to my cousin, other aunts, and myself. She told us that she was picking my grandmother up from work to take her to the hospital because her blood pressure was high. My cousin had taken me grocery shopping at Aldi in Salisbury. We were headed to pay for the groceries when we received the message. My cousin and I started talking because it was simply crazy that this was happening. We just had a major loss, so what now. After getting into the car, I had called my mom to see how things were going with my grandmother. She had picked her up from work in Milton and was headed to Nanticoke Hospital. I said, "Okay," and that I would meet them at the hospital.

I made it to Nanticoke before my mom and grandmother, so I decided to call my aunt and cousin just to chat until they arrived. As time went on, I realized it had been nearly an hour, and I had not seen nor heard anything from my mom or grandmother. I told my cousin and aunt that I would call them back; that I was going to call for an update. I called my mom, no answer. I called my grandmother, no answer. I called my aunt and cousin back and told them that it was weird because neither answered their phones. I then said that I would start driving towards Georgetown from Nanticoke to see if anything could have happened.

As I make it to the Exxon in Seaford, I get a call from a Lewes number. It was a Sunday, so I knew it could not have been a doctor's office calling me. I looked at the number for a moment and just answered it. I switched over from my aunt and cousin to see who it could have been. A woman was on the other end explaining to me that she was a nurse at Beebe and my mom and grandmother had been in an accident. I immediately pull over to the shoulder, where I started to tear up and ask, "Are they okay!" the nurse said, "Your mother asked for you. How long will it take you to get here?" I explained to her that I was in Seaford but on the way ASAP. I switched back over to my aunt and cousin and shared the terrible news I had just heard. We all got to the hospital as fast as we could.

My cousin and I arrived together and went in together. We went into the Emergency Room and waited for the nurse. She took us to my mom's room, and I was so terrified to look past the curtain. I had no idea what I was about to see. There my mom was just lying on the bed dozing in and out. She had seven staples on the right side of her head. When I went over to her and started talking to her, she woke up and was trying to move but instead started screaming out, "Ow, my chest! It hurts!" I did not know what was going on. Questions start racing through my mind like, "Are her lungs, okay? Is there something broken?" They had to give her something to calm her down because she would not stop trying to get off the bed. I was wondering what was going on with my grandmother because nobody had said anything about her yet. After the news I was about to hear, I wished I had not wondered so much.

The doctor walked in and explained that my mom had a bilateral fracture of her first ribs. This was why she was in so much pain. He then went to say the chilling sentence to my mom, "I'm sorry, but your mother didn't make it. I'm sorry." I was standing up but remember just folding up and falling to the floor, screaming yet again but this time even harder. The whole ER and probably the next floor could hear me, but I did not care. I was just told that my best friend was gone, forever. I could not wrap my head around what I had just heard. I immediately wanted to go and see my grandmother. When the nurse took me over to her room, I stopped in front of the curtain because I could not begin to imagine how bad my grandmother looked on the other side.

I peeked around the curtain after what felt like forever, and there she was, just lying there looking swelled up. Besides that, she looked perfect, perfect! She did not look disfigured in any way, so it was hard for me to believe that she could be gone. I sat in the room with her for a good while and held her hand. At one point, I rested my head upon hers and told her that I loved her. I even kissed the side of her head. Her hand was so cold and stiff. She hated to be cold, so I covered her arms just as she did for my aunt when she had passed.

I was able to stay the night in the hospital with my mom. Having to hear her cries and her saying over and over that this was all her fault, and it should have been her, really hurt me and broke my heart. All my mom was trying to do was care for my grandmother, and she had felt like she killed her on purpose. I spent the rest of that night preparing for how I thought my future would be, which would be taking care of my mom. I did not know what her mental state was about to be. I was okay with doing just that for her because she needed me. I owed her that respect after everything she has done for me and continues to do. That was one of the longest nights of my life. We finally made it home the following morning, and I gave my mom the best words of encouragement that I could at that time. My mother, grandmother, aunts, and cousin all taught me what strength is, so it was my turn to be just that for my mom.

My mental state and everything about me did not seem real anymore. I wanted to be dead. I was angry. I did not think I had a future anymore. All I knew was that I wanted to be six feet under so I could be with my grandmother again. I stopped eating and lost weight drastically to the point where I was 120 pounds. This was a weight I had never been at, even in middle school. Family, friends, and clients noticed the weight loss and started to be concerned. I would be so hungry, my stomach grumbling and all, but there was no way that my depression would allow me to eat. I honestly did not care. I was angry that my aunt and grandmother were taken away from me, especially at just two weeks and a day apart, like you've got to be kidding me. I hate the fact that my aunt and grandmother both went through so much in their lifetimes. How could a blood clot and a tree take them away from me? That does not even make any sense to me at all, man. The stories I heard about each of their lives would give me chills. I just could not believe they went through such horrible things but still ended up being huge blessings and sweet to others around them.

This is just the beginning of my healing process, but I will continue to shine and grow just as my aunt and grandmother always said I would. I will proudly make sure their names live on until after I am gone. Here are a few words of encouragement to my hurt self that should never be ashamed of what has made her stronger:

Dear T,

You are such a good-hearted and loving soul, which is amazing. Learn to be more selfish and put yourself first. There is nothing more important than the love you have for yourself or your own happiness. Right now, you do not understand because you are blinded and not too sure of your own worth. That is nothing to be ashamed of. This is nothing like you have ever experienced before, but no need to keep worrying because once you free yourself of all the baggage you have carried the majority of your life, you will shine like you never have, my friend. Then, you will understand and evolve into who you were truly meant to be.

I love you. Love you too,
T

CHAPTER FOUR

Abandoned, Molested, Alone...

Umunique Nevaha

I was molested by my uncle, someone my mother trusted, between the ages of three and four. I was not in a place where a three-year-old should have been. Things were all right for a moment, but after a while, things began to become weird. This man made me sit on his lap, and I had never done anything like that before. I thought it was okay, so I kept doing it. I did not know any better. It then progressed into him touching me in my private area. I knew that was not okay, so I would run and hide. He made me come back out into the living room while the music was playing loudly. He would discretely touch me while other people were in the room. I remember crying and throwing a tantrum. He would then send me into his room and let me cry myself asleep. When everyone had gone home, he would put his fingers inside of me and move them around.

My mother did not come back to pick me up that day. I spent the night with my uncle. He made me sleep in the bed with him. I cannot remember if anything happened while we were in bed together. The next day I woke up, and my uncle got me ready for my mother to pick me up. My mother did not allow him to give me any baths, so he just put my clothes on and sat me at the table to eat breakfast. All I could think about was how I wanted my mother to come and pick me up. I felt very uncomfortable. My mother finally arrived, and I thought to myself, "Finally, this nightmare is over."

My mother often asked me if I had fun while I was with my uncle, and I would tell her that I had fun playing outside. She never asked me about what I was going through inside of my uncle's home. The abuse continued to happen with this uncle until I was about four years old. I finally told my mother, and she did not believe me. She told me that I was a liar and she hated liars. She then beat me because she thought I was telling lies about my uncle. I kept crying and telling her that he did touch me, but she never believed me. I insisted that he touched me, and then she spanked me. Although my mother said she did not believe me, she never allowed me to go back to his house. As I look back on that experience, I think she believed that something happened to me.

I did not know what to think about this. My mom is supposed to be there to protect me and keep me out of danger. I believe that my mom should have expressed her love and embraced me. I felt like I did something wrong when she beat me. It made me feel like I was at fault for what my uncle did to me. My mother was and is a single mother who has been through a lot. She had her struggles in life while she was trying to raise me as a single parent. She was my mom. She was supposed to be there to protect me. The person who was supposed to protect me added to the pain I was experiencing.

My mother molested me with a baseball bat when I was five years old. Not only did I have to deal with the trauma my uncle put me through, but the person who I looked to for help was also hurting me. I had no one to run to for safety. I saw my mother being abused as I was growing up. I also saw her using drugs. I am not sure if her abuse of drugs had anything to do with her being abused.

I saw many things that a child should never be exposed to. I learned how to do a lot of stuff on my own.

I was eventually placed in a foster home. I felt the family I was with cared more about me than she did. So as days turned into weeks, I never thought I would see my mother again. I was okay with this. Other children were already at the house when I was placed there. I began to feel the other children didn't want me. I used to wonder if anyone would ever love me. I felt abandoned all over again. As time went by, I was called out to the family room where I saw my mother. I began to cry because I never thought I would see her again, and there she was.

I went back to my mother, and I was happy. I know that sounds crazy because of what she did. But she was all that I knew and trusted. As we got into the car, my mother started asking me a whole bunch of questions. She wondered if they were friendly. Did I have fun? Did I feel safe? There was not anyone doing anything inappropriate with me or mistreating me, aside from the first couple of days when the children were mean and did not want to play. I ate by myself, and they made fun of me.

I spent a lot of time by myself at the foster home, but eventually, the kids came around, and so did the grown-ups. My mother then asked if I wanted to go back to the foster home and said she would drop me off. I told her that I was not going back, and I wanted to be with her. Then she told me to act like it. I was at an age where I could express myself and explain how I felt about things. I guess this made her uncomfortable. She knew that if I did not mind telling her how I felt, I would tell everyone else. This was something that she feared. I think that is why she wanted me to keep quiet.

We stayed with my grandmother after I left the foster home. As time went by, things got better. I started to feel loved, the kind of love that a parent should give a child. Eventually, my grandmother began to care for me as my mother fell back into her old ways. My grandmother ended up passing away when I turned eight. Now, my mother had to care for me and my uncles and aunts. When my grandmother was placed in another home, my life became a living hell all over again. I knew once they were taken away that I would be next. Well, it was true. I was back in the hands of the Division of Family Services again. I was used to it because I knew it was either with them or staying with my mother. I chose to go back into the system. I knew that the social worker would take me to a home that I would love. I never got to go back to the same people that I was placed with the first time.

The house I was taken to was a lot better. There were just two other children and me there. I remember playing with the baby girl like she was a baby doll. I never got into trouble or yelled at. I never had to eat alone. It was always all of us like a family should be. I stayed there for two weeks, and then I was placed back with my mother. I was lost, scared, and confused. I struggled to understand why I kept being placed back in my mother's care. I did not understand why they would allow her to take me back. She abused me sexually and let others do the same.

As time went by, I was in the house alone, doing things that an adult should be doing. I had to cook for myself and get myself ready for school. I had to clean the house. I was taking care of myself by the age of ten. I had to grow up fast. I did what I used to see my grandmother do when she was alive. I used to help her cook, clean, and do chores. My mother would be gone for days and sometimes weeks at a time. I remember the power went out when I was home alone. I was in the dark for three days straight with no lights, food, or anyone to call on. I did not want to go to my friend's home because they knew I did not have parents.

They knew my mother did not love me. I had to find a way to do things on my own. I did not care if I was left in the home. There was not anyone there to mistreat me.

I went to school because that was where I could eat. I was on the complimentary breakfast and lunch program. I made sure to eat all my breakfast because I was hungry. I only ate some of my lunch. I would pack the rest in a small container and take it home to eat for dinner. I used to look for spare change on the ground to and from school to get food. That became my life. My mother finally returned, and the lights were put back on. She did not look the same. She looked a lot healthier. She went and got clean and was sober. She tried hugging me and telling me that she missed me. I asked her how she could miss me when she was the one that left. It was good to see her, and I was glad she was clean. I began to come around, and we were all right again. I guess she got clean because she had a boyfriend. I used to think in my head that I had never really seen her with a decent man before. I only saw her with men she did drugs with or men that beat on her. I thought maybe this man could work. I thought that we could finally have a real family, and I could have a dad. Then I used to wonder if that man would hurt me like the man did when I was younger. I told myself that he might be a nice guy. Well, come to find out, he was the best.

Three years later had passed, and I was thirteen years old. We moved from California to Utah. Everything was okay, and my mom was still with this man. My mom and I tried to have that mother and daughter relationship. As time went by, my mom broke up with her boyfriend. She went back to a man she used to date when I was a child. I was now fourteen, and her ex-boyfriend has come back into our lives. I was not too fond of it because I thought of her newer ex-boyfriend as my daddy, and he called me his daughter.

I immediately felt that she was going back to her old ways. I knew she would have men around and start doing drugs again. To my surprise, that did not happen right away. I brushed it off. I started dating a girl and did not know how to tell my mother. I knew that we did not have the best relationship, and she was with this new guy. One day, I told her about my girlfriend, and she was angry. She then told her boyfriend. I lost my mother for good after that. I moved in with my girlfriend and her parents. That was when my life started. I was now free of her. She disowned me and wanted nothing to do with me. She was out of my life for good. I finally got what I wanted, which was her gone. My life got better.

As I sit here today at 41 years old, I ask myself, why me? Why did I have to be the person to experience so many horrible things? I have been through so much trauma in my life that I must take medication to function. I suffer from post-traumatic stress disorder, anxiety, bipolar and depression. At 39 years old, I was on the phone with my mother. She told me that she was tired of hearing me cry. She told me to get it together and get over it. She asked me if I had taken my medication that day. She told me that she would not talk to me about anything until I took it. She also asked if I spoke with my therapist. I was driving and had to pull over. I could not believe this was coming out of her mouth. After I pulled over, I asked her if she knew why I took medication or went to counseling. She said, "No, tell me." I broke it down to her. I told her everything I had been through when I was a little girl. I also explained how the abuse she put me through caused me trauma.

Of course, my mother told me that she did not do anything to me. I was like, yes, the hell you did, and you need to own that shit. Then she told me that the drugs caused her to do a lot of things in the past. All I wanted was for her to take ownership of her actions; she refused to do it. I was like, it does not matter whether you were on drugs; you still did it. I told her to take responsibility for it. I explained that I was her daughter, and no mother or parent should ever do to their child what she did to me. She couldn't get the words out or even thought about saying sorry, and she still hasn't to this day.

I decided to forgive her, for me. People often ask how I can do such a thing if I were not the person that did this. I explain to people that the act of forgiveness was for me. Forgiveness did not take the pain away, and it still hurts. Forgiveness was the first step on my path to healing. I have the help of the All-Mighty God and my therapist. She is my life. She is my savior. Without her, I do not know where I would be today. I put her through the wringer, but she stuck by me every step of the way. It has been three years, and she has helped me regain the strength I used to have. I thank you, Dr. W, for everything. So, the question is, am I that strong woman? The answer is yes. But I strive every day to be an even stronger one. I will never give up on myself. I do not want anyone to experience any of the things that I have. Trauma was the worst thing that I ever experienced.

Dear T,

I want to start or by saying, I am sorry that we let things happen to us that are out of our control. But just know that you are a very strong little girl, and you will become an even stronger woman. As you grow more wise, you will turn into a beautiful black woman. If I can tell you one thing it would be that what you are going through is not your fault. I would also tell you not to blame yourself. You will have a son at 21, and he will not live for long. This will make you feel like your life is being turned upside down. As I sit here today, I try not to blame me. I love you and just know that I will never abandon you like everyone else has. I love you and keep striving to be a better you for us.

CHAPTER FIVE

Lost Child

Cheri Lee Fleming

I was a carefree timid, quiet, somewhat happy child who always did what I was told to do. I never knew what family love was. I longed to be a part of a family that loved one another. I loved being around my cousins because they treated me like I belonged there. They never teased or picked on me. I have always wanted to be loved by my family or have a family of my own to love. I now have a family that I love and would do anything for. I know that the way I was raised was not normal. I try hard to break those habits so that I do not repeat the cycle.

My story started when I was born, I do not know why it was, but I had a strong bond with my father. He knew it, and so did my mother. My mother was not too fond of the bond my father and I had. As I got older, I noticed that my sister got whatever she wanted, and she was very disrespectful at times. My brother was the youngest and was spoiled by my grandmother. That left me the middle child. I was just there. I loved my mother and grandmother, but my grandmother did not care for my sister and me because we were girls. She wanted a boy when she had my mother, and she made it known. My childhood is a little fuzzy because I have blocked it out of my mind.

My grandmother told my sister and me that she did not care for us. I believe that I was around six years old; she said if anything were to happen to our mother, she did not want us and did not know what we would do. What kind of grandmother would say that to her grandchildren? You would most likely be saying no one would, but mine did. I felt at that moment that nobody cared about me. My mother treated me like I was her stepchild. My father was not there. I had no one to talk to, and I pretty much shut down. I became frustrated. Nothing I did could change how I was treated. I did everything I was asked to do, and I was still treated as if I was not there. As time went by, my mother and father got married. My father was an alcoholic. I do not recall them arguing much. He drank and worked a lot. My mother worked as well. Shortly after they were married, we moved to my grandmother's trailer. It was tiny and became even smaller when we moved in.

My father had other children before my mother married him, three or four that I knew of. Things started going south for them. I remember going to see a little brother of mine that was not my mom's child. My dad started drinking more and staying gone a lot. There was a time when my father and mother were arguing. My father tried to hit my mother while I was standing next to her. I remember her grabbing me and holding me in front of her. Well, let's say after that, things weren't the same between them. After some time, I remember seeing their clothes cut up. They were cutting up each other's stuff. I believe my mother told my father to leave, and he did. I begged him not to go. He hugged me and left me crying. I was devastated because he was the only one who helped me while I was in school. I felt like my world ended a little bit. Well, that was when I started noticing that things were different between my siblings and me. My mother would tell me that I looked just like my ugly father. She said this so much that I asked her one day if I was ugly. I thought that I was ugly, and at times I still do. I had very low self-esteem as a child. My sister would always bully my brother and me until he stayed with my grandmother; then, it was just my sister and me. She would steal from me. I got in trouble for the things that she did. I was an honest child; I never lied because it was not in me to lie.

It seemed like I was criticized about everything. I remember singing my heart out, and my sister would tell me that I could not sing and to stop. I remember when my mom was working while my great aunt, who lived next door, watched my siblings and me. I felt sick. I stayed in the house and would not go outside to play. My brother stayed inside with me. My friends kept coming inside to see if I was feeling any better. I could barely move.

My mother and cousin came home from work and never said anything to me. Finally, my brother told her that I was not feeling well. I laid on the side of the tub as the fever burned me up. I thought that the end of my life was near. My cousin came into the bathroom and felt my head. She realized how hot I was and told my mom I was sick. She told my mother that I was ill and lying on the side of the tub to stay cool. My mother called my father to take me to the hospital. I remember my father carrying me to his car. I do not have a memory of anything that happened that day at the hospital. I can only remember the ride home. My father was saying something about my mother wanting sex from him.

My father was in and out of our lives, and my mother started dating again. There were some nice guys. If her boyfriends were nice to me or liked me, she would stop talking to them. I remember one of the guys that my mother was seeing. Things may have appeared fine on the outside, but something did not feel right about this man to me as well as my siblings. So I abided by a strike system. The first strike was when that man beat my brother. The second strike happened when he acted as if he was our father. The third strike was given when he touched me.

I was a very heavy sleeper. I slept so heavy that falling off the top of the bunk bed where I slept could not wake me up.

One night I woke up to my mother's boyfriend's tongue in my mouth while feeling him trying to penetrate me. When he realized that I was awake, he got off me. He put my underwear and pants back on. Before he put me back in my room, he made me touch his penis. I remember his hands rubbing all over me. At that moment, I wished I could go through the wall just to stop his hands from touching me. I do not know how many times he had done that to me.

One night he was drinking and took my brother with him to pick up my mother from work. When she got home, she told me to stay the hell out of her room. That was when I knew that night was not a dream. I realized that whatever he did was real, and my mother blamed me for it. She thought I willingly participated in it. The only people who know what he told my mother that night were my brother and my mother. A week later, she decides to make me go with her to take him back to his sister's home. She should have pressed charges so he does not touch another little girl. I find that very fucked up. Only God knows how many other girls he has done that too.

As time went by, my mother began dating another guy. This guy was very friendly, so my mom left me with him at times. It felt like a punishment because I stayed with this man while my brother and sister went to my grandmother's home. My brother played football there as my sister watched. I sat on the far end of the couch and cried silently while my brother and sister were gone. I guess my silence may have been loud because her new boyfriend asked me if I was okay. I managed to stop myself from crying so that he would not come out of my mother's room. After that, I never cried again until I became an adult. I cry now when I am frustrated and upset.

Growing up as a middle child that was not wanted was extremely hard. I chose to roam the streets, LOL! I spent most of my time outside, away from home. Staying away from home helped me to get into less trouble. It seemed like I was being blamed for things at home even when I was not there.

My sister would steal my mother's clothes and perfume, but I got the blame for it. I was a tomboy. I did not like girl's clothes. I felt like I was my sister's target. It was like she could not stand me or that she wished I was never born. I remember changing my clothes three times a day mainly because I did not like my clothes or that I got them dirty. I was not a picky person; I was very easy to please, but I was told at times that I was ungrateful. My mother has never said to me that she was proud of me for anything. I have been made fun of because I was fat. My mom never told me that she loved me. It hurts!

At the age of twelve or thirteen, I remember my mother sending me to a close friend of the family's home to help her out with her two boys. The oldest was a few years younger than me, and the youngest was about two or three years old. I spent the summer with them. It was hard but easy at the same time; It was easy because I was not home, but it was hard because the oldest would not listen to me. I tried to tell his mother, but he always made it seem like I was lying.

I remember one day, when their parents were working, the oldest invited some friends over. His friends held me down and took turns raping me. Some of them did not know what they were doing. They did not know where to stick their penis. I kept the incident to myself because I surely did not want to get yelled at like the last time I was raped. That incident made me keep to myself even more. This incident made me timid, self-conscious, and paranoid. Eventually, I came back home to stay with my mother because school was about to start.

I always did poorly in school. Most of my teachers noticed how quiet I was, but they knew that I was very smart. I did not put in the effort because I never got help at home and did not have faith in myself. My father would help whenever he could, but after a while, he stopped. He did not want to deal with my mother. I was a year behind in school. I was put in pre-first grade. The teacher would hit my hands with a wooden ruler for sucking my thumb instead of asking me to do my work. Finally, my mother came to the school to speak to the teacher about it. That was the only time I can remember my mom standing up for me.

Things were good until I got to the third grade. The teacher never liked me, and I barely passed. My mother and sister teased me, saying that I was trying to spell my last name, Fleming because I got all Fs. I truly felt lost in the world. I had no one. The fourth grade was a little better because I began receiving special education services. My teachers cared if I passed. It felt good to have someone care about me. I started hanging around people because their mothers treated me like their own child. It felt good to feel wanted. I felt like I mattered. I still do it today because I am longing for the feeling of being important and loved. I know that there is still a void that I carry within me. I still feel incomplete.

As I got older, I had problems sleeping, so I would listen to music. I loved listening to music and still do. I find myself singing songs that I listen to. I stayed out in the streets even while I was at other people's houses. When I graduated high school, I decided that I did not want to be home anymore. Working and giving my mom most of my money was not enough for me, so I went to Job Corps in Pittsburgh, Pennsylvania. I met new people. I realized that some people are not for me. I met one of my best friends, and things got better. However, I still was not comfortable sharing the things that made me who I was. As time passed, I still would not share.

One day I decided to share my life with one of my sisters and a friend. After returning from Job Corps, I realized my sister must have told my mother what I shared with her. My mother became so angry that she cursed me out. She asked me if those things happened, then why did I not share them with my father. I never had a phone number for my father, so there was no way to contact him back then. He rarely came around. I believe if I did tell him, he would have done something about it. He probably would have done something to my mother and the guy that touched me.

I shut down and kept it to myself. I stayed away from my mother's house when I came back to Delaware. I stayed with her for a little bit, but her boyfriend did not care for us. I had to get out of there. She expected me to be a maid while I lived there because I was not working. They tried to make me clean up after everyone in the home. I did not mind it too much, but she wanted me to get up and start cleaning at five in the morning. She wanted me to wash dishes and do laundry. It was hard to live there. I became depressed and tried to kill myself. I took my mother's heart medication and her boyfriend's prescription medicine.

It did not work because I am still here. My sister got her place and needed me to babysit. I went and was told that I was not welcomed at my mother's house anymore. So, I left and never went back. I found out that my father wanted to raise me, but my mother would not let him. I felt like I was not wanted or loved until my father told me that he wanted me to stay with him when I was a child. I realized that I was a pawn to my mother. I was used just to make my father unhappy. That made me upset because I could have had a better life. So, I stayed away from my mother. I never called, but I would answer when she called me. I love my mother, and I will always love and respect her.

I have gotten better at facing things that have hurt me. It took a very long time, but I still find myself holding back at times. I must remember that it is better to let it out than to hold it in. I know that it still bothers me because I have the urge to cry as I write this. Instead of crying, I hold it in. I know that it is not good to do that. Sometimes I tend to get upset or mad when I think about what I had to go through as a child. I ask myself why my mother did not believe me. It was devastating to feel that no one cared about what happened to me or rectified the problem. It hurts me to know that my mother was not there for me when I needed her. It is terrifying just thinking of the other girls that her boyfriend molested because no one did anything.

Sometimes I sit and think about everything. Sometimes guilt overtakes me because I should have done something. I also wonder how much accountability everyone would expect my mother to have for allowing it to happen. About fifteen years ago, my mother had a major stroke. It left her paralyzed on one side. It affected her speech and memories. Unfortunately, I will never get to ask my mother about any things that happened to me because she will not remember. I will never get to hold my dad accountable for leaving and not fighting for me. He died seven or eight years ago. I also will not hold my grandmother responsible for the way she treated us as children. She died six months before my father. I am a little upset with myself for not sitting down and talking to any of them about how I truly felt about these things. I feel like hearing them out would have given me some clarity.

My upbringing left me confused about how to treat people that I love. It left me confused about how I should allow others to treat me. I could have gotten the help that I am now receiving sooner. I would have healthier relationships with my intimate partners. As a result, I struggle to experience happiness. I realize now that no one can make me happy but me. Everyone should know that their happiness is dependent on themselves. I taught my children that the only way to experience happiness is to never give up on your dreams.

Dear Lost Child,

I know that things may seem complicated and that no one loves you, but you are loved and an intelligent person who always sees the good in everything and everyone. Never give up on hope nor love no matter what happens. You loved everyone, and you became an amazing mother. You learned that people are not perfect. As you get older, you learned to love yourself. You've become a strong, intelligent, successful person, so hang in there. Your best is yet to come!

Love,

Cheri Lee Fleming

CHAPTER SIX

Through The Flames

Olivia Janocha

You never truly realize the events that happen to you in life shape you into who you are. You will never fully understand the pain one hides beneath a smile. You will never truly see the story through someone's eyes. You will never get to understand the trauma in their mind. People deal with trauma daily. These traumatic events can affect people in so many ways; these experiences have long-term effects on individuals. They affect mental health, your view on life, trust, relationships, and your relationship with yourself. You may ask yourself, "How would she know this?" Well, because I am one of those people.

I can remember the things I had encountered at such a young age. Those are things no child should have ever gone through. At one time, I was just an innocent, sweet, and happy child. I was full of life and beyond happy! I was just completely innocent. As I grew older, all those things were taken from me. I never knew all my traumas would affect me the way they have.

When you hear your parents arguing nonstop, it really takes a heavy toll on you. Every day you wake up pondering, "What's next?" Was it going to be a good day or a miserable one? Would there be a family war or silence? You always questioned these things. I was so young; I was just a child. I should have been playing with Barbies, not worrying about arguments. The arguments that took place within those walls were hell. The screams screeched through the house like nails on a chalkboard. You were hiding underneath the covers to drown it all out and crying from the fear and shaking to feel something other than fear. You just never knew what was going to take place in that house.

As a child, I became anxious. My escape seemed to be my imagination. I would pretend to have friends. I would pretend to escape to another world. I would pretend to be okay; I would even have imaginary friends. It would take me away from reality for a split second. I would even hold onto a security blanket; it was my safety. When the arguments would happen, the house was no longer a home; it became a battlefield. The voices filled with hate and rage. There was anger in their eyes. That feeling was so very unsettling. I just wanted to run away, to escape. Quite a few times, I had tried. I would pack my clothes and toys in a "Power Puff Girl" book bag and run down the street. The fear of the unknown brought me back all the time, back to the fear of reality.

I played as a child. I had a couple of friends, and I did excellent in school. Then I would be home, and sometimes the days were good; other times, they were horrible. As a child, you do not understand everything that is happening. That is what I miss. You know everything going on is not all right, but you can escape more easily. You can run away into your imagination. You have an easier time not processing your trauma. Now I am 24, and it does stick with you. Everything sticks with you. It becomes a part of you. You just cannot escape it so easily anymore.

As a kid, I would put things away in the back of my mind. I could not process it then, but as I got older, I understood. My mind became a graveyard for dead memories. Those memories would slowly resurface. They were eating at me until there is nothing left. They were consuming my happiness, forcing me to process the past at that exact moment in such unhealthy ways. The unhealthy coping mechanisms began when I was a teenager.

The abuse in my childhood followed me into my teens. I began to understand then. I began to see what was going on now. I began to realize how horrible that home was. Arguing and family fights take a toll on you, especially dealing with it all the time. Watching your parents scream and yell at each other hurts. Watching them throw things at each other or chase each other around really messes you up in the head. I was a kid; I did not know what was going on. What did I know? I was terrified. Why was this happening? Why me? Why my family? Now, as an adult, I understand how badly this affected me.

I do not trust many people. I do not like to get close to people. I have suffered from depression and anxiety, and I have anger problems. I yell when I am upset. I would try to fight. I was once an aggressive person. I was afraid as a child. I was just so scared. I could not comprehend why all this had to happen. To be honest, I still cannot. My trauma did not stop at my childhood. Heading into my teenage years it got worst. As a teen, I began to process my childhood traumas. I began to understand what was happening around me. I could not hide the trauma in the back of my mind anymore.

I just could not mask it away. As a teenager, I could not put it away or hide it; I had to deal with it. I could not run away into my imagination. I had to handle it right then and there. My grandfather passed when I was fourteen. It was hard to deal with, and that is when my life began to go downhill. My father began to change, and so did all of us. The arguments increased, the tension rose, and the anger became stronger. It was a pure living hell. I was angry. As a teenager, my mood changed so much more than when I was a child. I was full of anger and rage. I hated people, I hated my life, and I would scream for no reason at times. I never understood why I was like that. My moods began to change my relationships even more. I had issues, and I just knew something was not right.

The relationship between my father and me became more challenging. It was not because I was a teenager now; no, it was far different. There was not much we could have done to fix it. My father was an alcoholic and stuck in his ways. That made him an angry person. He would strike all of us: my mom, my brothers, my sister, myself, and even the poor animals. The days were dreadful. I began to hate my life. I would never want to wake up. "Everyone, please just leave me alone!" was all I would say—lying in my cold, dark room, underneath that thick, black comforter. Just hiding underneath that blanket like it was my protection. I was shaking like a tree in a storm and feeling like there was a hole in my chest. I felt lost, confused, sad, and empty. Just wishing it would all go away or that I would go away. I would close my eyes, blast my music, and hope that when that CD album was done, the war would be over. Rarely was that ever the case.

If my father was not arguing with my mother, it was with us. Now that I was a teenager, I was able to stand up for my mother. When I would do that, he would target me. That was the beginning of my hell. This was truly my living hell. My house began to feel like a prison, my room the cell. I would barricade myself in my room, especially after my father and I argued. I did not want to be bothered. I just wanted to escape. When we argued, it was sickening. The things he would say were unimaginable: "You are nothing!" "You'll never amount to anything!" "I'm up here; you're down here!" Why would he say those things? Why would my own father say that about me? What made him so angry he just had to say those things? I was lost. At that moment, when he said all that, sadness consumed me like a fog. Then when it wore off, I felt numb. I felt nothing. I was a zombie. The way he said those words to me was like spitting vile. He wanted to hurt me, he wanted me to feel like nothing, and sure enough, he got what he wanted.

Those words stuck with me like glue. They stayed in my mind, destroying my happiness, and ruining how I felt about myself. I would never have thought my own father would hurt me in the ways that he did. The way his words affected me was unimaginable. They changed the way I viewed myself. I began to feel insecure about who I was. I would question my self-worth and even began to believe those things he said. Those things he said haunted me. No matter how much I wish I could forget them, I could not. My father hurt me with his words and actions.

Eventually, it became too much to handle. My problems were too much to handle mentally, and I began to target myself. School became difficult for me to attend. I could not wake up and go to school anymore. When I would try to wake up, it was like something was holding me back. I would get bad stomachaches, I would not be able to eat, and I would panic. I did not like going to school. I always feared something would happen or someone would target me. I knew I had anxiety. School was just too overwhelming for me. I hated going. I hated that feeling I would have when I would wake up in the morning. It felt I was being held underwater. It felt like I was drowning. I could not come up for air. My heart would race, my stomach would be in knots, and my mind would just wander. My traumas destroyed who I was.

My teenage years were the absolute worst. I would feel so overwhelmed with life. It was extremely hard to get through a day without feeling like I just wanted to fall down a hole and never return. I started self-harming when I was a teenager. The pain made me feel alive. The pain made me feel something other than being numb. The pain kept me alive. This was my escape. Self-harm made me satisfied. I did not know what that felt like as a teenager, but self-harm was damn near close to making me feel that way. Any minor inconvenience, I turned to a razor and drifted away into a wild, dark dream. When self-harm was not enough or significant events happened, I wanted to commit suicide. Multiple times I have tried. Once I did almost die. I remember taking the pills and throwing up constantly. My stomach was feeling like an acid pit, burning, and aching.

My best friend and brother drove me around to find charcoal pills to throw it all up.

I am not going to pretend like I was not scared because I was. I was terrified. I did not necessarily want to die. I just wanted the pain to disappear. Sometimes people who are suicidal seem like they want to die, but we feel like dying is the only way to escape our problems. Trauma takes a toll on a person. It makes you do things you usually would not do. It changes who you are in so many ways. It can truly mentally damage you. Between the self-harm and suicide attempts, it made me feel okay again. It made me feel like dying was the only way to be happy and make everyone else happy. I felt like a burden that I made everyone else's life completely miserable. I hated who I was. My self-esteem was so low. I felt horrible about myself. I felt terrible about the way I looked: "I'm too skinny!" "I have a big nose." "I look weird." "Who's going to love me?" "Who's going to like me?" Not only did I try and commit suicide and self-harm at the young age of fifteen, but I would also smoke weed and drink. It was my little escape from reality. It was my way to feel okay again--to feel "happy," to feel like somebody. Every day it was the norm for me to cut, drink, party, and smoke. It was the routine thing to do for me then.

Okay, so one thing added a lot to my habits and who I was. I was still so young. Even as a teen, the things I learned about myself came to me as a surprise. At the age of fifteen, I was in counseling. It was nerve-racking going through all of that. I hated going. I felt as if I did not need help. That I was "fine." Come to find out. I was diagnosed with bipolar disorder, anxiety, and depression. The doctor prescribed a lot of medication for me; it was unreal. Bipolar meds, anxiety meds, depression meds, mood boosters; yeah, it was a lot. I felt like a pill factory. Medicating myself with these pills made me feel ill. Some of the medicines made me worse, some made me sick, and some did not even do a thing. I hated taking medication. It just made me feel like crap. Was I always going to be on meds? Am I crazy? Why am I like this? These questions would always float in my mind. I felt different. I felt weird. I felt alone. Being bipolar was difficult for me. I felt like if people found out, they would judge me for it, that they would laugh at me like I was a nobody.

Having bipolar is like having an illness that taunts you. I never thought with having bipolar I would find "love." It was just this part of me I wanted to hide. When I found out I was bipolar, I realized there was a reason why I was so angry all the time—hearing my diagnosis pieced my behaviors together. To me, it was still overwhelming, but at least I knew why. I do not think I ever told my father until I was an adult. I felt as if he would judge me. I thought a lot of people would judge me.

My teen years were probably one of the worse experiences, as you can see. I suffered from a lot of traumas, abuse, pain, and misery. I let it all take over me until I did not know who I was anymore. I let it control my life. I let all that had happened to me take me captive and never let me go—serving me with the most traumatic life sentence and forcing me to "deal with it." Your teens should be for hanging with friends, being happy, getting dolled up for prom, or living your "best years." Not I. Nope. I was home in my cold dark room, blaring my music, staring at scars and a blade, and rolling down those grey and black sleeves, putting on a painted smile to hide it all.

I needed to hide from the truth and reality and hide from the pity of others. To hide from those damn awful questions: "Are you OK?" "What's wrong?" "Do you need help?" All more fake than my smiles. Well, what if I told you, I am not okay? Not like they would do anything anyway. Depression seemed to be my best friend. Every day we were together, stuck like glue. Wherever I went, so did she, along with her sidekicks' anger and anxiety. I could not wait to leave behind my teens. But why? It's not like my issues weren't going to find me no matter where I went. They always did. There was no sweeping anything under the rug because it all stood out. It would all continue to follow me around. I could never outrun it.

Flash ahead to year 17 when I began to venture into dating and boys, when I would try and talk to guys. I would always try to avoid relationships and guys in my early teens, I was 17. I was still messed up from all I had been through. Still questioning who the hell I was—still feeling insecure. I began to feel pressured to lose my virginity at 17. All my friends did; everyone around me did, so I should, right? So, I did. I did just that at 17. To a hook-up. Nothing special. Nothing sweet and comforting. Just a hook-up. That is how I knew I had a problem with love and guys. It felt like nothing to me, and at that time, I did not care. After that "hook-up," I walked home, the walk of shame. I hated that feeling; it made me feel worse about myself. That is when I became more promiscuous, hooking up, talking to guys, flirting. I became that girl. I was thinking at that moment that all of this was okay, and later knowing that it was not.

At 17, mid-year, summer of 2014, I met a guy. I chose to give a guy a chance to come into my life, to date me, and be with me not knowing the hell I was going to endure letting him into my world. To me, this guy seemed great, fantastic, like a gentleman. He was all I could have asked for. Boy, was I naïve! We began to date, and early on, I should have known he was no good, leaving me with his buddies at the racetrack to go home with his ex—my first legit heartbreak. The pain I felt, the hurt that consumed my body, the flashbacks of suicide and self-harm taunting me. I felt numb, weak, lost, angry, and confused. I felt worthless. The next day he came by, begging me to take him back. Of course, I took him back. Dumb. So very dumb of me. He and I had such a horrible relationship. Terrible. Dreadful. I cannot wrap my head around the fact I believed that was "love" that our relationship was my view on "love." Because it, sure enough was not.

The few years we were together were hell. We had our good moments, of course. But the bad conquered the good. The bad was always there. We would argue so much! I did not know what love was, nor did I know what a healthy relationship was. The version I had on "love" was my parents arguing and fighting. To me, it was okay to argue.

Those arguments were normal. Later to find out, no, it was not. I cannot remember much about the good times we shared, but God, I could write a novel about the bad times. Our relationship was so unhealthy; it was almost unreal. I stayed so long that I allowed that guy to hurt me the way he did. Dating that guy was like willingly taking a toxin and putting it into my body. You know it's terrible for you, you know it could kill you, you know it could harm you; but you still do it regardless. Dating him was like asking for your life sentence; you feel so controlled, so stressed, and you just cannot escape. That love was your prison. You cannot escape no matter how hard you try. You are stuck, stuck in that cell, hoping to find a way out before it's too late.

I was afraid, but it was almost like I was addicted or attached to this guy. I just could not get away from him. I stuck with him through everything. Regardless of how it hurt me, I stayed. Talk about self-harm. Loving him was self-harm. Loving him was no good for me. But I still let him do what he did to me. At first, the verbal abuse was yelling at me, putting me down, the name-calling, the hurting me with his words. I felt like he was crumbling me down to nothing. At this point, my self-esteem was at nothing. Zilch. Zero. Again, I felt worthless. I felt as if I was the problem. As all of this was my fault, I felt that maybe I am just not capable of being loved. That is when the physical abuse came into play. It was the grabbing, the pulling, the pushing, oh, and the spitting.

Sometimes I would stupidly fight back, willing to try and protect myself. But I knew he could overpower me. Those flashbacks in my mind would pop up, and the fear would flow through me. That is when I would try and protect myself. I did not want to be my mother.

I wanted him to see me at least stand up for myself. Even though he would always win, he would tell a fake sob story to sleep with someone. I will never forget this day, February 14th; it just always stands out to me. You know February 14th, Valentine's Day, the lover's day. Right? Well, we had just broken up a few days ago, and I had bought him tickets to a concert for his birthday. Instead of taking me or giving me the tickets, he took another girl. Of course, that made me so very upset. So, on Valentine's Day, he showed up at my house, arguing with me and starting a large fight because I mentioned to him about paying me back for the tickets. He took the money from his jeans pocket and threw it at me like I was a stripper. He told me that I was a hoe and liked it when he threw money at me.

I got upset and began to yell at him, which made him furious. He chased me out of his truck, and straight up hit me. He gave me a clean punch, bruising my cheek. Until this day, he still denies it. He has always been such an evil person. I just was stupid enough to allow him to hurt me. I allowed myself to take him back even after all the lying, cheating, beatings, and backstabbing. I let him guilt trip me into giving him sex. I allowed him to hurt me beyond measures.

Another day I remember was New Years'. His friends were throwing a party. We were invited, so we decided to go. Well, I got extremely intoxicated. I began to feel sick, so my boyfriend at the time, and his buddies, rushed me to the bathroom. My boyfriend exited the bathroom for whatever reason, and this boy walked in. I was so drunk, so when he began to touch me, I could barely even fight him off. He was feeling me all over; even though I kept saying "stop!" he just kept touching me. I remember telling my boyfriend, and he did nothing about it. Nobody did. So, I never looked at it as a big deal. I just brushed it off. Boy, was all that a slap in my face.

I honestly should have known better. I should have known he was going to hurt me. This was my first relationship, first love, my first everything. And all he could do was hurt me. He destroyed who I was. He destroyed my view on myself and men. He made me feel like it was all my fault. I began to feel like total crap about myself. When he would flirt or cheat with other women, I would compare myself to them—searching up their Facebook or social media—just staring at their picture and wondering, "Why her?" Was she prettier than me? Is she better than I am? Like what made him do this to me? All these questions would float through my mind. They ate at me. They were making me feel so low. He made me feel worthless. That was something he was good at. He made me feel like I was nothing. I felt useless, like a failure. I hated the way he made me feel, but I still stayed.

I still stuck with him. I still let him ruin me. I do not know why I did that to myself. Why did I let a guy overpower me? Why did I let him hurt me? I let him pull me apart like a Jenga tower, pulling at me until I crumbled down lying in the aftermath, scattered, and abused. I was often left contemplating why I stayed and why I could not leave so easily. Being in a toxic relationship is horrible and so confusing. It takes control of you; you allow one guy to run your life, taking you captive. I did not know how to leave; it was like I was attached to him.

Part of the reason I stayed was that I did not think anyone would want me or love me again. I was like damaged goods. Who would want a girl that has been hurt so many times? Also, he was great at manipulation. He would be so good at these fake apologies, and I was so real at forgiving them. He knew how to make me forgive him. He knew all the right things to say. He knew exactly what he was doing to me. He was so good at manipulating me. He made me believe he loved me and even talked me into having a baby with him. I gave in. I gave in to his pleads, and we ended up having a child together. I will never regret my daughter. She has made me who I am today. I love that little girl to death! What I truly regret is her father.

I promised myself not to give my kids a dad like I had, and I failed. The way her dad treated me before, during, and after pregnancy was horrible. The pain he gave me. The hell he put me through. The trauma I had because of him. I was just a young, naïve girl looking for love, and I found it in all the wrong places. I had one of the worse experiences being pregnant with our daughter because of him. He would leave for weeks at a time, be with other women, go to parties, and get drunk. He would block my calls, so I could not call or text him. He would only come by to fake a check-up on me so that he could hook up with me. He never cared about our baby or me. He was just a sex-addicted narcissist who only cared about himself. He would have other girls message me attacking me. He would be in secretive relationships behind my back. He caused me so much misery. I was pregnant, and he still did not care.

I remember this one time he took me to Wawa so I could get food. I saw on his phone flirty messages between him and another girl. Of course, I was upset, so we argued. He yelled at me to "Get out!" and made me walk home at 2:00 AM, pregnant. He was so unhealthy for me, and I still stayed. To this day, I still do not understand why I allowed that to happen to me. I would never, ever, ever let a guy treat my daughter like that. Ever! So why did I stay? Why did I keep going back? Why did I keep making an excuse after excuse for him? I was just blind in "love," I guess. I let this person ruin me to no extent. I let this guy take advantage of me because I chose to think he loved me.

When we had our daughter, he left me when she was only a couple of months old. He left like it was nothing. He moved on so quickly like it was the easiest thing for him to do. He began a relationship with a girl, and in no time, they were married. He was pure evil. The way he acted was repulsive. He would call me and harass me, and so would she. They made my life extremely miserable. I was so naïve; still, I would make poor choices, I would go out, and I still tried to find love. I felt unlovable and bad about myself.

First my dad, and now him. I felt so low about who I was. I flirted with guys just to feel "Okay" about myself. Being a first-time mom and going through all of this was so very overwhelming. I hated how everything was at that moment. I wished it would all just go away, but sadly it never did. It just kept getting worse. Even when we were broken up, he still made my life a living hell. He still tried everything to hurt me, and he succeeded. He and his wife would disrespect my daughter and call her names. They would come to my house and try to fight me. They would do anything in their power to hurt me. It was horrible. It made me feel sick the way they would treat me and especially our daughter. I do not know with whom I had a child because he is so full of hatred. He is like the anti-Christ, just so full of evil and hate. He was full of deceit, greed, and so egotistic. He thought he was superior, and he's just evil and angry boy, a boy who is not capable of knowing how to love. I do not understand how I allowed someone like him to break me down to just dust. He kicked me around like a soccer ball. He walked all over me like I was a damn doormat. Never again!

Now here I am, 24 years old. A survivor! I know what I have been through and understand it, trying my best not to let all of this affect me anymore. But it still does. It is hard just to let it go. I would be lying if I said it was easy. I sit every day and think to myself, "Damn, you have been through a lot!" And I have, but you know what? I am stronger than my past! I am better than what I have been through! I got through some of the worse times in my life, alive and okay. I walked through the flames of my past, hurt, and burned, but alive. Breathing. Able to tell my story. I did it! I walked through it with some scars, but that is okay. The scars are my battle wounds. They remind me of my strength today. I am grateful to be here and tell my story and laugh with my friends and family, to be able to have the most precious daughter and be with her! To be able to come home every day and hold her, play with her, and laugh with her. I am so happy I lived through my traumas. I am happy I got through trying to take my own life. I am proud I overcame self-harm. I am grateful I got away from my abusive, toxic ex. I am thankful my other relationships did not work out.

I am beyond happy to be working on the relationship with myself finally. That is the important one. Truthfully, how can you give love to someone else when you cannot even love yourself? That is probably why my relationships fail. I never loved myself the way I should have. I never gave myself the credit I deserved. I pushed guys away because I was terrified of love. I did not think I truly deserved love, and I did not think they would treat me right, so I pushed them all away. I was afraid of guys, still kind of am. I know they are stronger and more powerful than me. But I am working on it. I am working on Olivia. I am trying my best to make myself happier, more trusting of others, more accepting of myself, a better daughter, a better sister, a better friend, and most importantly, trying to be the best damn mother I can be! I want to guide my daughter through her life, catch her when she falls, hold her when she is scared, protect her from her fears, and teach her from my experiences. And to love her like no other!

Today I am learning. I am trying to love myself more. I am trying to build my confidence up. I am beginning to understand my self-worth. I am proud of who I am. I came a long way, and I am never going to stop. I will always be a survivor and a warrior. One of the most significant battles in my life, I overcame! I am a warrior! Where there is no struggle, there is no strength gained. In that case, I should be the Hulk by now. I am not my trauma. I am not bipolar. I am not my past. I am Olivia. I am strong. I am caring. I am powerful. I am beautiful. I am worthy. I am loved. I am not what happened to me. I am the rainbow after the storm. I am the sunshine after a long rainy day. I am that extra nugget in your meal box. I am me. I could move mountains if I wanted to. I can change the world with progress. I can genuinely help others. There is no force more beautiful and powerful than a woman determined to rise! I will rise through everything. We all will.

Dear Liv,

I'm going to begin by asking, "how are you?" I know things are tough. I know you feel as if the world is against you. I know you don't feel like holding on any longer. I know you are tired of the arguments, tired of the fighting, and tired of the stress. I promise you. It will get better; it does get better! You are so incredibly strong. You hold a power nobody else does. You are a unique, beautiful, and courageous soul. You are you, and that's what makes you worth everything. You have people who love you and cherish you! This life is a wild one, especially what you have dealt with. I am telling you the future is bright. You'll have a daughter, and you will love her like no other. She will be the one who picks you up when you're down. You are her hero, and you will do anything/everything for her. Life is tough, but you are by far tougher. Stop letting people get to you; it's not worth it. You are too smart for all that. It's hard not to listen to what they say, but they are unhappy with themselves. Don't let how someone feels about themselves tear you down.

You are a skyscraper; nobody can touch you. You rise up through it all, broken and bruised. Your life serves a purpose here, so do not give up. You will be happy, I promise you. Life may not make sense to any of us, but keep pushing through. Do not stop, run, keep fighting! You will be everything you've ever imagined and more. You will be powerful and so strong. I have seen it; you just wait until you do. I wish you would've just not let so many people get to you; you would've been so happy! You could've done so much more if you just didn't listen to the negative things others had to say. Everything happens for a reason, though, and I'm a strong believer in that. I wish you wouldn't let others walk all over you; you're not a doormat; you are a woman. Nobody should treat you the way they have, but what can you do buy become stronger from it all? You will make it through. You will be happy. It takes time and patience. There is a light at the end of the tunnel. Just know I'm proud of you always, and you should be of yourself also. Keep fighting and holding on!

You are stronger than your past. Never forget that. Never give up on yourself. You will be all right. It takes some time, but you will be okay. Love yourself. Do not doubt yourself. We will all be okay. Take a deep breath, step back, and relax. We did it. I did it.

~Liv

CHAPTER SEVEN

TAKE A LOOK BEHIND MY MASK

Jas

Thoughts and Murmurs

Shut up! Be quiet!

It's not our turn

You must be seated

This one needs me

So you have to wait your turn.

Hide behind this mask

I will come back for you.

That person needs me to be there, don't you see!

Our cousin did this – whoops, dismiss

That person needs me to walk with them; they can't get through it alone

Dreams are haunting me—whoops, dismiss

That person needs me to beat the odds and be their saving

grace – so hold on, I have to listen.

Numbness is overtaking us – whoops, dismiss

Who am I? I don't know,

But I know what THEY want me to be

So don't you see - Self- Smile and be pretty

Others need me, so let me be.

                                        - Jas Seals

Jumping out of my sleep, sitting straight up, eyes wide open, panting and sweat seeping through my Barbie nightgown. Overwhelmed by the dream I just had. It's pitch black in my Barbie room. All around me, Barbie this, Barbie that. Barbie borders that you peel and stick to the wall, Barbie curtains for my one window in the corner, Barbie doll head on my dresser, Barbie sheets and covers on my bed. I was eight years old; what else can you expect. I laid back down on my Barbie pillowcase, staring out my bedroom door.

I knew it was still dark outside because I could still see the nightlight shadow in the hallway. My room stood overlooking the stairs; then it was the bathroom to the left of my room, my sissy's room, and at the very end of the hall, my parents' room. It was the perfect house for my family and me, very warm and welcoming. But this night, I felt scared and alone. I tried to shut my eyes to think of happy thoughts, maybe a cartoon I saw earlier or those funny Junie B Jones books, but I failed. The dream was racing through my head so fast. It was like the trains I see every day on the bridge outside of my house. I could not just cry; I was wailing like I was just spanked on my booty.

How can I have a dream about this or him? This is wrong? I'm not supposed to even see this. That is, it -- I need to be spanked! My parents spanked me every time I did something really, really bad. So still lying on my soaked and wet pillow with tears still falling, I start screaming at the top of my lungs, "Mommy, I need a beating, I need a beating, Mommy." Repeating it over and over again for somebody to hear. The next moment I hear my parent's door fly open because it squeaks, and I hear heavy footsteps on the wooden plank floor coming straight towards my room. In a blink of an eye, my mom is in my doorway. She flips on the switch. I can tell she is really upset because her eyebrows are down, little triangles have formed on her forehead, and her eyes look tired. She says, "You want a beating? Okay," She snatches the covers off of me, which left me exposed.

Her hand is lifted; I already feel the sting before she hits me.

I close my eyes; I can't watch

1...2...3. Aaaahhh!

1...2...3. Sting!

Yelling in distraught to the top of my lungs

1...2...3. Owww!

1...2... 3. Psstt!

Trying to catch my breath, now I'm coughing and crying at
the same time.

1...2...3. Aaahh !

1...2...3. Aaahh!

She yanked the covers back over me, turned off the
lights, and said, "Now go to bed" while closing my bedroom
door this time. I heard her footsteps going back down the
hall to her room. I simply yell out "Thank you, thank you," and
"Thank you for that," through my tears and the burning mark
left on my body. She has done what I asked. I rolled over to
hold my pillow, closing my eyes, whimpering, with my
breath slowing down. I was asleep again.

Sitting Indian style on the floor, with Legos scattered
all around I talked to my favorite doll. "What should I build
for you, Princess, a castle or a boat? You already have a
castle upstairs in my room, so I'm just going to build you a

boat instead." I am working on building my doll baby the best Lego boat, and then my cousin appears. He is standing over top of me. My cousins are here visiting my family, so my parents left them in charge while they stepped out.

"Do you want to play Doctor?" my cousin asked nervously.

"Sure," I said happily.

"Okay, let's go upstairs to your room," he said.

I really did not want to go all the way upstairs; I usually don't go upstairs until it is about my bedtime, and that is no time soon. I just had lunch.

"Okay," I said simply.

He quickly walked up the stairs holding the rail. I could not go up that fast; I was only four. I could not even reach the railing; I had to use the wall underneath the railing for my balance to climb the steps one after the other. My room was the first room to the right. My cousin was already in there with my play stethoscope around his neck. I jumped into my room so excited and ready as can be to play. I only play at school with my friends or with my family when I see them. I have a little sister, but she is still a baby, and she does not do anything but cry all the time. I never played this game before, so I was so excited. My cousin closed my door. I was so happy and ready to play that I did not think that was suspicious.

"Okay, stand in front of the door so that I can check your height," he said in this deeper tone, trying to sound like a doctor. I did what he said and started to laugh. He sounded just like my doctor. "Mmhmm, very good," he said.

"Now, let me see your wrist," he said. I gave him my wrist. "Everything sounds normal. Now get on the bed," he said in a playful tone.

I ran over to my bed and tugged on the bedspread like I do every time to help me onto the bed. As I was about to ascend my cousin said, "You have to take off all of your clothes just like at the doctor's." Of course, Jas, as I said in my thoughts. I let go of the bedspread and removed all my clothing quickly to get on the bed because I was cold.

I remember going to the doctors in the past; the doctor would give me a small nightgown to put on. My mom would be there for the exam. I climbed on top of the bed and laid flat on my back with my hands by my side. My cousin was quickly taking off his pants, and my mind started to wonder. I was no longer cheerful and happy but uncertain. I could not connect this emotion because I never felt it. I was lying there on my back exposed with nothing on and cold because the AC is on. This fantasy doctor role-play is not how a normal trip to the doctor goes. I trust my cousin, though, so I just lay there my heart racing; my palms are close to my side, and they feel so heavy.

My cousin got on the bed and said, "Let me check your heartbeat." He put the earpiece from the stethoscope in his ears and placed the bell on my chest. Then his other free hand moved to the other side of my chest. He slid the stethoscope down to my belly button, and his free hand moved from side to side. At this point, I could feel my heart beating really fast and butterflies in my stomach. I never felt this way before, and I remained quiet. I looked at my cousin for guidance on how I should be playing this role or what to do. His eyes never met mine again. He let out this sigh that overwhelmed me, and my body stiffened. I saw he dropped the bell of the telescope that was in his other hand, and he had it in his boxers. I was very confused why his hand would be in his pants. My cousin got on his knees on the bed and wiggled off his boxers, and out came a little worm that I never saw before.

My body was still motionless like I was on an operating table. It felt wrong to look, so I looked to the wall that was to my right. On the wall hung a beautiful picture of a little girl kneeling to pray on her knees by the bed, which actually looks like my bed. To her right was a shadow of Jesus sitting on the bed, being there for her as she prayed. On the same picture, it was words that read, "Mommy said: You always know just what to do - And that I should put my trust in You - and then - Mommy said When she's out of answers she talks to you - So that is what I'm gonna do!" While I was lost in the picture, I could feel my cousin flip over my left hand and put something slimy in there and made me squeeze it. He kept sighing, but I never turned to look. He then went to the end of the bed and parted my legs, and everything was quiet.

I am not sure what he was doing. I was just lost in this picture. I never noticed the teddy bear in the corner of the little girl's room. I wonder if Teddy sees the shadow man. Then I felt something grab something inside me that I have never felt before. My heart stopped, and I became uncomfortable. I shifted a little but not much to make a difference. Then he just rubbed my insides with his finger. I had those butterflies again and then crept a sound I never heard before from my own mouth. Sort of like a groan, but I'm not sure what it is. Still never looking down there, my eyes were just fixated on the picture. I wonder if the little girl feels the shadow man while she is praying. My cousin lifted my legs and scooted a little closer, and then suddenly, the door flies open. My head turns earnestly to the door. In the doorway stands my babysitter, our older cousin. The doctor jumps up and rushes to put on his clothes. I sit up with my heart racing from his reaction.

My older cousin is yelling, "What are y'all doing in here?" "Playing doctor," I blurted out. My cousin ran out of the room once he was dressed. My older cousin just looked at me. My older cousin walked over to the bed, picks my clothes off the floor, and puts them back on me. We both said nothing. We heard a loud noise from somewhere in the house, so she immediately ran out. I hopped down off the bed and went to play with my Barbie princess castle that was in the far-right corner on the other side of the room.

I picked up my Barbie doll and walked her to my Barbie princess house and thought Barbie won't mind. I played there for a while until I heard the front door slam and a bunch of yelling. I went to my bedroom door to peer down the steps. I could not see anybody but shadows. The people were not in view, but they were angry and loud. It made me uncomfortable my heart was pounding, and I had these butterflies in my stomach again. I closed the door and went back to my doll Barney and to cook him some play food to eat. As I was sitting Indian style fixing Barney food, another cousin of mine came in and just looked at me. I looked at her and went back to playing. She asked nervously, "Are you okay? And my response was "yes" per usual when anybody asked me that question before this time and even after. Then my thoughts went back to my other cousin. Why did he run out of my bedroom earlier? Was I not playing the right way? I then asked my older cousin, "Where is my other cousin? "My older cousin said, "He did a bad thing, so the aliens came and took him." I nodded my head while feeding Barney. That makes sense in my head since we heard that loud noise. My older cousin turned and left, shutting the door leaving me to myself.

One hot June afternoon has been affecting me for more than 20 years. My cousin tried to commit suicide that day for touching me. When the grown-ups heard about the "doctor" role-play, the attention was focused on him. My parents said they did not notice any changes or different behavior from me. They decided not to talk with me about it. They thought it was best when I was older if I had questions about what occurred, I would come to them about it, and they will tell me. Having that dream for the first time when I was eight years old still was overwhelming and still overwhelms me to this day. I can still feel the lump in my throat and the tears burning my face.

I did not receive many beatings or spankings when I was growing up through the years. I only received them if I did something bad. So, receiving the spanking that night solidified my own thought; I was wrong and disgusting to think of those thoughts. That was my first and last time ever asking to be spanked, but my mask started forming. My parents were going through a lot in their own lives, and I felt as though my problems were minute, and I could fix them myself. Besides, I was their sunshine baby that was no problem for anybody to watch. I was very independent and easygoing. This is what everybody said that knew of me. So let me just smile and be pretty. I cannot let the world see I have issues was my motto growing up and even until now.

The evil of that role-play paved role-plays to be a safe haven for me. I would long for the days of playing dress-up with my family and pretending to be a famous singer or superstar. I could not do that for the rest of my life, so I started exploring my creative talents through writing. It paved the way in the fourth grade for me to go to college in the summer. I was acknowledged in eighth grade for having one of the best creative writings in the school. I earned a partial scholarship to study abroad overseas. I told myself over the years that I had forgiven my parents. They did what they thought was best, and they were going through their own tribulations too.

About two years ago, I wrote my cousin a letter explaining how his actions impacted my life. He apologized and stated that a person did it to him too. I love my family, and I love my life. I was lost in the darkness a few times, but I had many successes and have seen many wonders that some people only dream about. I will not say I am totally healed. I am still in counseling, trying to figure out who I am stripped down without the trauma, or the expectations put on me by other people. If I could impart one piece of wisdom to the person reading this, it would be to listen to the things that are not spoken.

Hey Sunshine,

I am proud of you! You did the best you could by yourself. Now is the time to unpack everything that is burdening you and welcome those who God has sent to help you. Thank you for not giving up but finding a safe haven in being creative or the arts. You are special, and God has a lot in store for us. So, hold on tight as we ride this out together.

love you so much,

  Jas

CHAPTER EIGHT

In The Dark, Trying To See The Light

Jada Harper

I have faced a lot in my life, but my main issues are my learning disability and depression. It all started when I was born. I entered the world on January 24, 1999. I was a premature baby born at 28 weeks, weighing 2 pounds 1 ounce at birth. Being born so early caused me brain damage, which is the reason I have seizures. My seizures caused my learning disability.

In first grade, I had a seizure that changed my life a lot. I still remember that day even though I was so young. We had a school assembly that day. After the assembly, our teacher let us go to the bathroom. I remember going into the bathroom stall; after that everything was black. My teacher realized I never came out of the bathroom, so she got someone to check on me. The nurse came in and saw

I was having a seizure, and I was taken to the hospital. They do not know how long the seizure lasted, but it had to be long because of the amount of brain damage it caused.

When I went back to school, I remember not understanding a lot, especially math. Teachers, and people in general, throughout my life have always been impatient with my learning disability. A lot of times you can explain something, and I still do not get it. Due to my learning difficulties, I had two paraprofessionals when I was in elementary school. The first para I had from kindergarten to second grade. My first para was not very nice to me. She would yell at me when I would struggle with my classwork. It made me feel uncomfortable when she would yell at me, but I never really said anything to her. I would go home and tell my parents what she would do.

My mom had to advocate for me a lot in school. Before entering third grade, my mom wrote a complaint letter saying I could not work with that para anymore. That is when I got my second para. I remember feeling relieved I would not have to spend another year with my first para. My second one was so nice! There were maybe a few times she got frustrated with me, but it was rare. I sometimes felt annoyed having a para because it made me feel different from my other classmates who did not have one.

As I transitioned to high school, I did not have a para working with me. I remember at first being happy because I felt I was finally like an ordinary student in school. However, that happiness soon turned to fear. I was so used to extra help I started to struggle in school a lot more. Teachers often called on me to answer questions. When teachers would call on me, my heart would race, or my stomach would ache from being put on the spot in front of the whole class. Often, I got the answers wrong, and teachers would say that I was not trying or paying attention.

My classmates often asked why I could not understand the work. When I reached seventh grade, my mother found a better school for me. I graduated from Positive Outcomes Charter School. I felt much more comfortable at that school. Most teachers had the patience for my learning struggles. My learning is not just hard for me in school but just life in general. I must have my parents help with a lot, and I cannot make decisions for myself. I feel no one understands a learning disability unless they have been in my shoes. I sometimes think if I did not have that seizure in first grade, my life would have been different. The trials that I have experienced make it difficult for me to understand my purpose.

Before understanding I had a learning disability, I was happier. I used to have specific career dreams, such as being a doctor, which would be difficult now with my situation. However, I have a new career goal of working in childcare now, so it does not bother me at al. The most challenging part of my learning is my mom always having to explain it to people. I feel people think it is an excuse when I try telling them myself. Also, it's challenging not being able to make my own decisions, most people my age can. If I did not have a learning disability, I would feel like a normal adult. My learning is trauma because I do not feel like a normal person. What I liked about myself before discovering my learning disability was my happiness.

My second trauma experience is depression. The cause of my depression has two reasons. My learning disability is one, but the other is feeling like I am not good enough from a break-up. I dated a guy in 2018 who made me feel worse about myself. We met at Walmart. He was a cashier and asked for my number, and we started talking from there. I felt shocked and happy I got a guy's attention. I remember feeling nervous he would lose interest. As I grew more paranoid, I told him my fear, and he promised me that would not happen, and I believed him. Nothing could prepare me for what was going to happen a few months later.

The third month into the relationship, I could tell he was losing interest in treating me well. He began to look like he was not happy to see me, and he was not affectionate with me anymore. Usually, he would kiss me when he would see me. He stopped doing that. I remember slightly joking one day. I told him that someone does not want to kiss me anymore, then he kissed me, but the kiss felt fake. Later that night, he came by my house again, and he looked upset. I asked him what is wrong? His response was nothing. I knew something was not right because of the way he was treating me. I remember going to bed that night. While I was lying in bed, tears were flowing down my face. I did not know what I did to make him lose interest in me. I had guesses as to maybe why. One of my guesses was my learning disability. I told him I have one. I thought perhaps he saw my struggles and lost interest due to it.

However, the reason he did not want me anymore was for a different reason. He finally told me on a warm evening of June 25. We were sitting in my living room. I remember my heart racing because I did not know what he was going to say. His exact words were, "I like my lady to look sexy for me." That sentence plays in the back of my head every day. He said it was because of my clothes. I knew he was losing interest, but I would never have thought it was over the clothes I used to wear. I mainly would wear jeans and a T-shirt around him. The day I met him I had on jeans and a T-Shirt. I asked him if I was cute the day we met. His response was yes, but I could have been cuter. He even said I could get ideas from my mom on how to dress sexy. He also stated I had low self-confidence. The reason he knew was that my mom told him. He said he likes a confident woman and someone that turns him on. He knew I struggled with believing in myself, and he continued to talk down to me. I did not say much. I just listened. I was so heartbroken. I did not know what to say. I always think if I was not his type, why did he approach me? After he broke up with me, he made me feel so bad about myself I decided to change my style of clothes. I used to love wearing T-shirts. I stopped wearing them because they brought back the hurtful things he said to me.

I remember deciding to change my style four days after he broke up with me. I got rid of a lot of my T-shirts, mainly the ones I wore around him. I begin to obsess over buying new clothes, hoping and thinking a new guy will like me. I went into my closet and picked out something I usually would not wear often. It was a dressy top. Wearing something other than a T-shirt felt different but good because I thought this was the only way to get a guy to like me again. I wore all my dressy clothes at home and when I went out. I wore them home even though no one could see what I was wearing. I wanted to feel good about myself. I still do not wear T-shirts at home today, but I do not wear my dressy clothes home anymore. I try to save them for when I go out.

As long as it's not a T-shirt, I am okay with what I am wearing. I tried wearing a T-shirt again, but I could not do it. When I wear one, I think about the painful words he said to me. I wish he knew the pain he has caused me. It sometimes takes me two hours to decide what to wear because of all the things he said to me. That year I cried over him so much. I remember constantly wondering if he had a new girlfriend. What I found out soon made my sadness worse. My best friend told me that she saw him on a date with another woman. I cried that whole day. I did not think it was fair that he could start a new relationship so fast while I had to suffer feeling lonely and impossible.

I thought he was out of my life for good at that point. In 2019, a few days after Valentine's Day, he texted me out the blue saying Happy belated Valentine's Day. I instantly felt angry and confused. I did not think that he should contact me after hurting me the way he did. We argued back and forth through text messages. The next day my mother tried getting him to apologize to me. He refused and did not think he did anything wrong. I told him I never wanted to hear from him again. I blocked his number. That incident made me feel like I was not good enough. Even though I changed my style of clothes, I wonder if there was something more?

During the first year of the break-up, I noticed that my sadness was beginning to turn to anger. I mostly cried when I felt lonely. I prayed every day that the right man would come into my life one day. I sometimes blame myself for what happened. I think if I had dressed cuter, then maybe I would still have a boyfriend. The good thing from this break-up was learning his true colors. I learned in the end what type of person he was. You can think you know a person when you do not. It is hard to believe he is the same guy I met at Walmart. The day we met, I would have never suspected him to be the person he turned out to be. When I look in the mirror, I am okay with what I see. I sometimes wonder if I am beautiful enough to be loved again. I know many people experiencing the love I want, and it makes me wonder why can't it happen for me?

I want marriage and kids one day, but sometimes I fear that it will not happen. As each year goes by, I feel time is ticking away, and it will never happen again for me. What made me happy before my bad break-up was believing I would experience the love I wanted so bad. When it did not happen the way I hoped it would, I was left feeling depressed.

My sadness has changed my relationship with my family and friends. Sometimes when I get sad about my loneliness and break-up, I become distant from my friends and family. I do not want to bother them with my drama, but I do feel I need to let it out and talk about it with someone. I think one of my friends does not understand. She always says stuff like do not focus on guys, or take a break from trying to find love. I feel it is easy for her to say that because she is in a relationship now. When she was single, I think she was more understanding because she knew what loneliness was like then.

When my break-up first happened, I did not just become distant from people but places too. I avoided going to the Walmart where my ex worked. I would ask my mom to take me to another Walmart. I could not risk running into him. I felt it would be awkward. Maybe not for him but me since I was the one that got hurt. Also, I thought I would burst into tears if I saw him. I wanted to be with him. One day my mom went to that Walmart without me and asked someone if he still worked there. She found out that he was no longer working there.

At times I feel sadness and anger. Other times, I feel at peace. My distraction is music. I love listening to and writing music. I like to write about what I go through. I handled my break-up by writing about it and changing the way I dress. I honestly would not do anything differently. The process I went through has made me feel better, however, when it comes to my appearance. I do wish I did not cry over him as much as I did. I honestly would rather be angry at him than to be sad wanting him. All I want now is someone better one day who can make me forget my pain.

This experience was traumatic because of how it affected my self-esteem. I titled my chapter "In the Dark Trying To See the Light" because both experiences put me in a dark place, longing to see the light. Sometimes the light is visible when the depression is not bad. I have good days and bad days.

Dear Jada,

Be prepared for life, knowing that you will face some hard times, but you can make it through it all. You will have always have a learning disability and will experience some bad relationships. Although you will experience many things, I want you to know that you will be left standing in the end.

CHAPTER NINE

Suicide:
The Unexpected Death of a Parent

Sara

December 29, 2014 is a day that will forever be ingrained in my soul. The day of the week was Monday; the weather was cold but sunny. I even remember what I was wearing- a black Gap hoodie, a light washed pair of skinny jeans, and a black pair of UGGs. I was at work laughing with co-workers and had just finished eating lunch with my supervisor. I received a call on my cell phone from my mom and did not hesitate to answer, as my mom and I regularly talked throughout the day. I assumed my mom was calling to ask me what I had for lunch or to make plans for us to have dinner later that evening. I quickly learned that none of those scenarios was the reality, as she was not initially speaking when I answered the call but breathing heavily as if she was in distress. She said, "Sarah, I'm hurt, and I need you to come to my job right now." I kept asking her what was wrong, what happened, and her response was, "Just come to my job, right now," and then she disconnected the call. My mom rarely calls me by my name but instead by my nickname, which reaffirmed in my mind that something was seriously wrong. My supervisor and co-worker were standing beside me when I received the call and instructed me to leave and go immediately to my mom's job, which was less than five minutes away.

I do not remember exiting my job, but I do remember hurriedly racing to my mom's and the unbearable thoughts that were pacing through my mind. I thought, "Was my mom attacked by a client?" "Did something happen to my sister?" "Did something happen to my grandparents?" "Is my mom sick and in need of urgent care?" The thoughts were never-ending. My anxiety was at an all-time high as I began praying to God and the universe for everything to be okay. When I arrived at my mom's job, I ran up three flights of stairs to the third floor. As I entered the office door to the section that she works in, I observed that every door to every office was closed, which was odd. My mom's supervisor met me at the door and escorted me into the conference room. Upon entering, I saw two police officers and my mom with tears streaming down her face, cheeks flushed red, her breathing staggered, and her head was lying downwards on the table. I began asking her and everyone in the room, "What is wrong? Are you hurt? What is it?" It was at that moment, with pain-filled eyes, that she locked eyes with me and told me, "They found Edward dead today. He killed himself."

Edward was my father and my mother's husband. During the drive to my mom's job, I had not considered that the emergency was related to him based on the dynamics of our relationship at that time. A barrage of emotions and memories began flooding my entire body, many of which had remained dormant for years. I felt tremendous guilt, but I knew that I had to find a way to be present and in the moment for my mom. My mother began crying hysterically and reached out for me to hold her. I immediately started crying, and as I held my mom, I became so overwhelmed with emotion that I began vomiting in the conference room. Once the regurgitation of emotions and grief momentarily subsided, I started asking what happened to him. One of the police officers stated that when he did not show up for work, his co-worker went to his home and found him hanging on the door, dead. An autopsy would be completed, but it appeared that he committed suicide. I asked if there was any note, and they stated a note had not been found.

The expression of emotions and feelings has been a dauntingly arduous task for me since early childhood. Anger and satire being the exceptions and ultimately becoming my default modes of expression throughout life until this point. I was forced to face the grief of losing a parent unexpectedly and death by suicide. This event opened the gateway for so many unanswered questions, seemingly never-ending grief, guilt, anger, resentment, and so many emotions that I cannot articulate even to this day.

Processing the aftermath of emotions presented following my father's death was one of the greatest obstacles I have encountered on my journey in life. I was simultaneously engaging with my siblings, uncles, and relatives, who began traveling to Delaware upon hearing the news of his death. I was internally going through memories while dissecting the history of the relationship between my father and me, trying to answer questions that were never answered and ultimately determine if I attributed to him ending his own life. I watched my mother, the stronghold of our family, unravel emotionally day by day. I watched her blame herself while trying to understand why the person she had known for over half of her life would end his life without even reaching out to her one last time. It was heavy, and for an emotional avoider like me, there was no escaping the sadness.

Due to the manner of his death, my mother could not immediately identify the body until the swelling of his head subsided. I did not want to be a part of that process. My uncle accompanied my mother when the time came. His body could not immediately be released until an investigation was completed to confirm that his manner of death was suicide. During this time, my father's youngest brother and wife arrived, followed by the middle brother and then the eldest. My father was extremely close with his three brothers, and although they could go long periods of time without seeing one another, their bond was unbreakable. Immediately, two of my uncle's expressed doubt in the legitimacy of my father committing suicide. They expressed their concerns with the police department. Specifically, they requested that my younger sister's mother be investigated. We learned he messaged her at 4:45 in the morning that he killed himself, asking her to tell my sister that he loved her. That was questionable to my uncles because out of all the people in my dad's life, no one understood why he would contact the person that seemingly cared about him the least. The eldest brother believed that he did kill himself based on my father leaving a Bible open with a specific scripture circled related to redemption that was found when my mother and uncles went to clean out my father's home. His death was ruled a suicide, and no further investigation was conducted. Two of my uncles still have a hard time accepting that my father, the strong one of the pack, raised as a devout Catholic, would kill himself.

My father has a total of five children. I have three older brothers and one younger sister who was four years old at the time of his death. I received a great deal of scrutiny from my siblings, specifically my youngest older brother, as he blamed me for my father's death due to my father and I not being on speaking terms at the time of his death. The cause of this was an incident that occurred one year prior in which my dad and I were in a physical altercation. My brothers did not understand why my father and I did not get along. I was the lucky one that he had raised for most of my life in their mind. I internalized their emotions, their grief, defended myself enough to end the conversation, but I refused to engage in a battle that would create division amongst my siblings.

The reality was that none of them knew who my dad was or what kind of parent he was to me. The same brother who blamed me was the only brother who witnessed the dynamics of our relationship over the years, yet he chose to ignore history and use me as an emotional punching bag to heal the pain that he was feeling. To this day, he still attempts to engage in the same toxic behavior. He was the closest to my father. He had lived with my father as an adult. He was aware that my father was battling demons that many were not aware of or chose to ignore. On the surface, he was working and personifying the image of a productive member of society.

My brother knew that my father was an alcoholic, and that he blamed himself for an accident that happened with my brother when he was younger, where a grenade exploded in my brother's hands, causing him to lose several fingers and have long-term medical problems. He was also the victim of physical and sexual abuse. He never spoke about it, but one of my uncles confided in me when explaining some of my dad's trauma in life. The reality is that my father had become an alcoholic isolationist who had gone through life hurting people because he had been hurt in life. Maybe those who only knew him over the phone never experienced that side. Perhaps the siblings he grew up with were never exposed to who he was with those closest to him as an adult man, father, husband. The truth was I had my own conversations in my head daily, nightly, replaying conversations, replaying good and bad memories of my dad, asking myself, could this have been prevented? I blocked out everyone else's opinions. I focused on supporting my mom and began working on how I would overcome not only his death but the way that he chose to die without enabling the emotional repercussions to have a long-term negative impact on my life.

To complicate matters more, two days after my father's death, I had another lifetime surprise when I discovered I was pregnant after being on birth control for over five years. Although I was in a relationship with the father of my child, I never wanted children and had done almost everything in life to prevent any possibility of me procreating. Although I was unsure if I would move forward with the pregnancy, I knew I could not drink my feelings away or engage in recreational activities that involved putting any drugs into my body until I decided. I was at a place in my life where those leisure activities were a norm, so the process of grieving was even harder, as I was forced to deal with raw emotions. I felt utterly trapped and alone as many did not understand the complexity of the relationship between my father and me, nor did they know I was pregnant.

The funeral was not scheduled until January 10, almost two weeks after his death, due to the investigation's delays and having the body released. I took a month off from work, and during that time, I tried to self-process every aspect of the death and life of my dad. I thought about my dad hanging himself on his door, leaving the dog to watch him die. I thought about him not reaching out to anyone besides my sister's mom, his childhood traumas, and learning that he had been on a downward spiral for the past three months, according to his employer's. Both jobs stated he kept going to work intoxicated and being sent home. Also, when my uncles and mother went to his home, it was filthy. This was all extremely out of character, as my father's main job was a government job, where he had worked for almost 15 years. He was a man of great order and organization.

His pension was vested, and he rarely took a day off. He was a supervisor and had always been a model employee. If you knew my dad, you would know how extremely clean and borderline OCD he was about the cleanliness of his house and car. He would make you take your shoes off when you came into the house, and he never left trash in the trashcan. He even made people take their shoes off when they stepped in his car. He was undoubtedly on a downward spiral, and the reality is that no one was there to catch him. I had not reached out since our fight, and he had not either. Although my mom and dad were still legally married, they had been separated for the past ten years but had remained best friends. My father would become angry and disrespectful towards those closest to him. He pushed people away, so it was normal for people to go for long periods of time without speaking to him. I knew he battled his own demons, but I never once thought he would let his demons consume him.

I have my share of good and bad memories with my dad. I have memories that will remain locked away in the hidden, unspoken chambers of my mind. I know that I learned more about him in death than I ever did in life. He had been living with me from age seven until sixteen, yet as an adult, we had no solid bond or sense of loyalty like a father and daughter should have. There would forever be unspoken truths that shifted the dynamic of our relationship. He dealt me some of the greatest heartbreaks up until the very end of his life. The reality is that there was a great deal of pain behind the anger and resentment that I felt for my father throughout adolescence and into adulthood. After the first two years of him moving in with us, he stopped showing me that he cared or loved me; in fact, he consistently demonstrated the opposite, unless he was drinking, and even that was based on his mood. He was never a protector, a provider, the father that would meet my first boyfriend and lay down the "laws of dating my daughter." He did not even attend my high school or college graduation or send a congratulatory message. But no matter what our relationship had endured, I never would have wanted nor predicted this outcome.

At the end of the day, he was my father, and I wish I had reached out to show him that I still loved him despite everything, that as I was going down my own path of self-destruction, I was becoming so much like him. I wish that I could have accepted my father for who he was before he died. I could have shown him unconditional love and not based my expectations and acceptance of him as a father on what I wanted, but instead on his life experiences. If I had adopted that mindset when my dad was still alive, I would not have been hurt by specific incidents. I would have interacted with him in a manner that was more conducive to us maintaining a healthier relationship, which could have ultimately saved his life.

Once I made it through the viewing and the funeral, I knew it was time to begin strengthening my mind to return to work and continue life without having these open emotional wounds created while grieving. The never-ending thoughts, memories, what-ifs...I knew I had to silence those before I re-entered society. For the past month, I had rarely left my room and the house unless I did something for the funeral. I had limited my interactions with people unless it was with immediate family members because I did not want people to see me upset. I processed my grief alone. I had conversations with myself that I could never have with my dad and closed the door once I felt peace. I also knew my mom was having a tough time coping, and if I were still grieving, it would upset her even more. I chose to accept everything for what it was, let it go, and never speak about my dad or his death again.

I knew that when I returned to work, many people would speak and ask questions, as my dad was well known, and many co-workers attended his funeral. I knew I had to be emotionally strong enough to answer the questions without crying or becoming upset or allowing any questions to trigger memories that would impact my day. I prayed and told myself I would not be a victim of the situation and that I would not use this as an excuse for continued bad behavior.

I thought about the life inside of me and about crossing over the bridge of motherhood. If I chose to do so, I knew I had to begin locking away any traumas from my past so that it would not inhibit my ability to be a good parent. I have continued not speaking on his death or our relationship until writing this narrative. Every year around the anniversary of his death and funeral, my siblings and relatives always have these collective phone conversations about his life and death. I choose not to participate.

Since my father's suicide, I have been told that I have become more emotionally distant and cold. I think I am just afraid of losing someone suddenly without any explanation again, but I do try to make a point to tell people I love them frequently. I check in on all my family members at least once a month, even if, for whatever reason, we are not on the best terms. It took three years after my dad's death before I drove by his house or by the convenience store that was his part-time job. In the relationships that I've had since my son's father, I do not speak about my dad, only that he is no longer alive. He must visit my son in his dreams because, although I never talk about him since the age of two, my son has spoken about his Pop Pop Edward and how he is in the sky watching us.

I am not one to indulge in the belief of spirits, but how can I not believe in some spiritually transcendent and celestial moment when I know we do not speak about my father around my son. Yet, with solid conviction, my son knows his name and is so familiar with who my father is or was. I guess life is funny like that. Initially, I would tell my son it was a dream and dismiss it, but now I embrace it a little more and remind him that he is so unique that he has his own guardian angel that visits him personally. My interpretation of his appearances with my son is that my dad tells me he is watching over me and my little one, and that he forgives me, and he knows that I forgive him. My son is, without a doubt, here for a reason. His life is bigger than mine. Every day I am reminded of the amount of joy and love that he brings to my family.

I have watched my siblings and my mother constantly go down the rabbit hole of grief, trying to understand why my father did what he did. I have watched family members self-destruct, allowing their pain to eat them alive. The irony in his death is like his father; he died alone, with the cause of death also being self-inflicted, an important factor that no one in my family discusses. So naturally, as I am going through the stages of grief, I began questioning my future. Will I end up like my dad? My answer will always be no, and that is why I have chosen not to speak on his death for so many years. The misunderstood mind will never be understood in death. I do not want to waste my time trying to understand what others perceive as a mystery when I believe my dad is at peace. He was a tortured soul, and I hope that anyone in life feeling that lost and tormented shares those emotions with their family and friends and receives the help they need before it's too late. My dad pushed everyone away, people who would have done anything to reverse this outcome. He leaves behind him broken children, siblings, and a life partner, all of whom will be forever impacted by the unexpected and traumatic way he died.

I choose to continue moving forward with life as time waits for no one. I choose my son and his happiness, strength, and well-being over anything. I choose happiness and peace of mind. I choose to live a purposeful life, with love being the driver. I have no doubt that everything I have endured has created the platform for the woman I am becoming and destined to be.

If my dad is out there listening, I want him to know the following:

Dear Dad,

I remember when you taught me how to play Chess. I remember when you ignited my interest in old black and white films and old movie classics like Clash of the Titans, the Odyssey, Coffee, and so many more. I remember when we would watch baseball for hours together. I remember your sense of humor and how much you loved mom; you just did not know how to love her in the way that was needed for your marriage to work. I remember how much you loved your mom, your brothers, your kids, and how you were trying to be a better father to my little sister than you were to us. I remember how much we look alike and even walk alike. I remember your smile and your laugh. I remember you putting olive oil on all your food and us laughing at you. I remember you calling me "boo"; sometimes, I hear someone calling me that, but there is never anyone there. I remember our sundae parties for New Years'. I remember you always telling me, "It's the Rican in you," when I would lose my temper or order a bunch of tropical foods that nobody but us would eat. I remember getting toasty with you and the first time we took the magic carpet ride together, lol! I remember you training Smokey and ordering him burgers with no bun or condiments from Wendy's. I remember spades nights at your house and endless laughs all night. I remember all the good, too. I may not speak about you, but I remember you, the good in you. I really do wish I could have saved you. I forgive you, and I will always love you.

Love,
Sarah

CHAPTER TEN

Love Isn't Supposed To Hurt

Amanda Grant

I remember the day as if it were yesterday. July 4, 2013, was his birthday. As soon as he walked up to the counter at my job, the smell of alcohol hit me. A few months prior, these two boys came into my job. I was 18 and working at Burger King. I had been working there since before I graduated high school. I was not putting too much thought into it, being as though I was trying to get money. He and I would flirt with each other from time to time. It just so happens that he kept coming back, and we would start to talk more and more. He was just so fine, and his smile, the deepest dimples, was just my weakness. He came into the restaurant drunk on his birthday. It was just something about him. When he asked if he could have my number, I gave it to him. From there, we started talking on the phone and hanging with each other.

We started dating and spent all our free time together. I remember the first time he told me he loved me. Although it seemed a little bit too fast, it was just something about the way he made me feel. I always had these butterflies when I was around him, talking to him. He made me feel beautiful, wanted, and cared for. I just wanted him. I loved him. It wasn't until months later that things started to change.

It was Easter Sunday, and I had just gotten off work. His mother lived down the street, so I decided to go to her house. I was always spent most of my time between my apartment and his mother's house. When I got there, he was sleeping, so I woke him up and told him that I was going to my aunt's house for dinner. Everything was okay, but later that day, I had run to the store with my sister. When I got back to the house, my aunt told me that my boyfriend had called. I grabbed the phone and called him back. When he answered, something just seemed off, but I did not know what it was. Everything had been so great. He started to yell at me and asked me where I had been and what I was doing. I was so confused because I woke him up before I left to tell him where I was going. He told me that he would see me when I got back.

Eventually, I got back to his mother's house, and his mother answered the door. She said I do not know what you and my son are arguing about, but you got to get your stuff and go back to your apartment. Even though I was confused and upset, I grabbed my stuff and started walking down Main Street to go back to my apartment. As I was walking, I saw him on the opposite side of the street coming from the opposite way. We made eye contact. Although we both smoked weed. I was not familiar with a lot of other drugs, but the way he just looked confused told me it was something else. Yet, still not knowing what was going on, we started arguing about where I had been.

Something just came over him, and he punched me in my eye. My eye was swollen and black. It was in the afternoon on a busy street. He pulled me behind one of the buildings and started yelling at me. He did not realize people saw the incident happen, and they called the cops. When the cops pulled up behind the building, he started running. I just stood there, not knowing what to do. The cop came up to me and asked what was going on. He said that a few people had called in about an incident. I played it off, being as though I did not want my boyfriend to get in trouble. I did not know how to process the situation.

I told the cop that some random guy just came up to me and hit me. Eventually, they found him by his mother's house. He was arrested and taken to jail. The cop asked me if I had somewhere that I wanted to go. The only person I could think of was my aunt. The cop took me to my aunt's and explained what happened.

She took me to the emergency room for treatment and to ensure the incident was documented. I was reluctant to answer questions because I did not want the incident to be documented. Right before leaving, a nurse came in and asked if I wanted to take a pregnancy test. I said, sure, why not. I did not think that I was pregnant, but I took the test anyway. I could not remember missing my period. A few minutes later, she came back and said that it was positive. I was speechless. I did not know what to say or do. My aunt heard the whole conversation. She started talking about the option to adopt and blah blah blah! I did not want to listen to that shit. I did not want to hear anything, to be honest. I was just so confused about everything that had transpired, and now I was pregnant.

I stayed at my aunt's for two days and then went back to my apartment. My boyfriend was still locked up, and I did not like being at my aunt's. I called his mom and told her I needed to talk to her and asked if I could come by. She told me that was fine. When I got there, I did not know how to approach the situation. I knew he was still locked up, but I needed her to know that I was pregnant. She and I were not very close initially, but I went ahead and told her anyway. Her only response was, "Ain't no baby gonna keep no man." I just stood there, not knowing what to say. I was trying to process what she had said. I knew what she said was true, but on the other hand, I thought him putting his hands on me was just a one-time thing.

I wanted my baby, and I was young and did not have much family. The family I did have was not close at all. I thought everything was going to be good. I loved this man, and I wanted to have this child with him. While he was locked up, we talked on the phone. I stayed at his mom's house, so I was not by myself. His best friend came to check on me while he was locked up. We were all friends. I was not sure why his best friend checked on me so much.

After my boyfriend was released from prison, he started to make assumptions about me sleeping with or kissing his best friend. I never did, but the argument started to get heated, and he kept asking me. After numerous times (more than I can count), I finally said, "Yeah, I kissed him." Even when I told the truth, he did not believe me, so I just said I did it because I was frustrated. That started more problems between him and me. He begins cheating on me, and I could never understand why. I had not done anything wrong; at least, I thought I did not. I was still so in love with him and thought that we could work it out.

At the start of my pregnancy, we struggled financially. We rented a room, and he walked me to work every day. Finally, after saving enough money, we could get a one-bedroom apartment on the other side of town. That is when things started to get worse. He began smoking dippers or wet. I never knew what it was until he explained it to me. I was so turned off. He was the man I loved. I could not understand why he would do those things. It started with him getting high sometimes, then started doing it every day. We would get into arguments about it every day. Throughout the pregnancy, I was cheated on and lied to. One day he kicked me off the bed while I was pregnant. I still forgave him because it had been a while since he put his hands on me.

December 26, 2014, I had our precious baby boy. I finally thought things would look up, but it only got worse. He was getting high every day while also selling drugs. I helped him to sell the drugs as well. I was still working every day. I will never forget the day I walked in from work, and he was higher than I had ever seen him. He had a gun. I cannot remember what we were arguing about, but he threw me against the wall and told me to open my mouth wide. He stuck the gun in my mouth and said, "I should blow your brains out right now, you stupid bitch!" I could not yell for help. There were three other men there while he was doing this. They were trying to get him to put the gun down. I stood there frozen, in shock. Tears just started falling from my eyes. I felt helpless. I did not know why this was happening to me. They finally tackled him for the gun, and I just quietly went into the other room. I cried and cried. Things got worse. He was still getting high. He bit the shit out of me, burned my clothes, and tried to throw me out of the window.

I started smoking and drinking every day. I was tired, but I still wanted to work things out. I thought things would change. We were struggling with money, so I started writing fake checks and cashing them. We spent the money on the bills, diapers, clothes, and anything else we needed. I knew it was wrong, but I did not stop. This went on for months. I wanted to stop because I did not want to get in trouble, but it was too late. There was already a warrant out for my arrest.

I got arrested on my 21st birthday. I will never forget that day. I was there all day waiting for someone to post bail for me. I was sitting in the cell thinking about how I did not want my life to be like that. I was not made for prison. I realized that I was the one that put myself there. Finally, my boyfriend and his family posted my bail. I felt relief when they picked me up from the precinct. I knew it was not over. I eventually would have to face a judge in court for my crimes.

After I was arrested, it seemed like nothing got better. I started working two jobs, and I did not get to spend time with my son. I was depressed and often felt as if there was no way out. How did I let things get so out of control? A few weeks later, I had to go back to court. I originally had 33 felony charges. The public defender was able to get it down to three. I was left with two forgeries in the second degree and one theft of a senior. I knew what I did was wrong. I did not know how I allowed myself to get into that much trouble.

The relationship between my boyfriend and me was still rocky. We were always on and off. The cheating never stopped, and the beatings continued. Things just seemed to get worse. November 22, 2017, was a day that I will never forget. My life changed forever. It started off as a normal day. I worked the night shift. After I got off the next morning, my boyfriend's sister and I ran some errands. We were trying to get ready for his mother's birthday. I took a shower when I got home. As my boyfriend was headed out the door, I remember telling him to "be safe." I am not sure why I said that. Every other day when he would say that he was headed out, I would just tell him that I would see him when he got back. Anyway, he said okay, then closed the door behind him as he left.

I was exhausted, so I fell asleep quickly. I remember hearing loud banging on the door. I looked over at the clock and realized it was about 8:30 p.m. The bedroom was located next to the front door, so I asked who it was banging on the door. I heard the voices of my boyfriends' mother and sister letting me know it was them, so I opened the door. I was still very tired, so I went back into the bedroom and fell back asleep. As I began to dose off, I heard his mother scream out "Call an ambulance! He is not breathing!"

I was confused and began to panic. I searched for my phone and found it on the charger. It was off so I had to turn it on. I called 9-1-1. I ran out to the living room and there he was. My boyfriend was lying on the couch unresponsive. The dispatcher asked me if I knew how to give CPR. I told him that I did not know much about how to give CPR, but I was willing to try. I was told to take him off the couch and to place him on the floor. I did not think that I could lift him alone, but the adrenaline that was shooting through me proved otherwise. I laid him on the floor and started CPR. I was pushing on his chest, and I heard a faint breath. I was still pumping his chest until paramedics walked in.

His sister came in and gave me a look that I had never seen before. It was like she knew that he was gone. After the paramedics arrived, I was still thinking that everything would be fine. I told his sister to help me get the baby dressed so that we could be with them at the hospital. Just as we were about to leave the bedroom, the paramedic walked in and said the words that no one ever wants to hear. "Sorry Ma'am, there is nothing else that we can do." Chaos immediately erupted within my home. His family members began to show up. Everyone was crying.

The next thing that I knew, I saw the paramedics bring my boyfriend out of the house in a body bag. As I am watching all of this happen from across the street, I fell to my knees. Two of his cousins tried to hold me up. I was so weak in my body. I was inconsolable. I remember screaming "Not my baby, not my baby!" I could not handle it.

The next week I did not eat, nor did I shower. I lay in the bed. We all knew that my boyfriend had to have taken some sort of drug. We just did not know which drug it was. It seemed like everyone had different accounts of what happened that night. The autopsy came back about a month later and revealed that there was PCP, fentanyl, and marijuana in his system. His mother had the funeral for him in New York where their family was from.

After my boyfriend's death, life was different for me. I had to figure out how to adjust to this new life with just my son and me. His father will never be in his life and sometimes that's difficult to think about. The memories can be daunting and debilitating to the mind. I have blocked out the memories that were too painful. I have tried my best to grieve and allow myself to experience healing.

Hey You,

It is currently May 29, 2021, and you are 26 years old. You have three handsome boys and are an amazing mother. I know that you are young, and things are tough. You may feel like things will never change. I know that there is a lot of heartache and worry that you may carry, but things will get better. Find yourself, love yourself, and most of all, be strong. You got this! There will be times where you think that you can not handle what you are facing. Trust me girl, I know that you can. You can do a lot more than you think. You are brave, strong, caring, loving, wonderful, intelligent, and you have the biggest heart out of everyone you know. I know right now you just have your baby boy, but you will have a set of twin boys and all your children will be a blessing to you. God made you their mother for a reason!

Amanda

CHAPTER ELEVEN

Men Like Him Prey On Women Like Us

Amber Graver-Roof

If you do not recognize him when you see him, maybe my story will help you, and you will be smarter than I was. I had just gone through a divorce after ten years. I had three small children and found myself stuck in a state where I had no support system. I am from the Midwest. I came to Delaware on military orders with my ex-husband, who was on active duty for the Air Force. There are not many options for women who divorce the military and are stuck in foreign places because they share custody with their ex. You cannot take your babies back home with you. You must find a way to survive on your own.

I was working long hours at a dead-end job. I was submitting application after application, trying to get myself in a better position. My boss Tommy jokingly said one day, "if I looked like you, I would be sitting on a yacht somewhere and have a sugar daddy." I laughed and responded, "I have been married my entire adult life. I have not been anywhere. I don't think becoming a hooker is the answer to my problems." The next thing I knew, I was creating a profile on a sugar daddy website. This was after I was convinced that a sugar daddy was just a rich boyfriend that would help you get by. A sugar daddy understood that some women were not financially able to be a "contributing partner." If you are willing to date them, they're ready to immediately begin fulfilling a "husband" role in some aspects and make sure the lights stay on.

Before I knew it, someone had responded to my profile. I was nervous but curious at the same time. I was shy with men, and I had not had any experience dating as an adult. He had been messaging me for well over a month before I decided to have lunch with him. I missed our first date because I was so nervous about meeting somebody new. When I finally did meet him, I was surprised at how charming and sweet of a person he appeared to be. I guess I was expecting some disgusting pig. I did not think any worse about myself for even considering the arrangement, but I did not expect to meet somebody "normal" like him. He was great. When he told me about his love for children and his involvement with the church, he just seemed like such a loving and wonderful person. I was impressed by him. He was witty, masculine, kind, and compassionate. He was one of those people with such an attractive personality, you meet them and see all their physical flaws... but then they become beautiful. You see "them," not just their "shell." Our physical appearance is just a shell covering our souls. True beauty lies in the heart of the soul.

He told me that he would normally never do something like this, and the only reason he was not traditionally dating was that he was married. He told me they had been separated for five years and lead separate lives. He told me that his wife had a series of affairs over the years while he remained faithful. He said that he was tired of being alone. She had moved on and had a serious boyfriend that she was focused on. They had not been intimate in years. He referred to her as "more of a business partner." I told him that I was not judging him for his situation but would not date a man who is still legally married even if he had been separated for years. He told me that he was ready to start dating again, and he would go ahead and file the papers.

By the end of the first date, I realized that I liked him. I was a little ashamed of meeting him online on such a sleazy website. So, I declined to enter an "arrangement" with him. He looked a little confused and said, "You don't want me to be your sugar daddy?" I laughed and told him, "I'm sorry, but I wasn't expecting you to be wonderful. You seem like a genuinely nice guy, and I don't think that you need to pay anybody to spend time with you." I meant that too. There was nothing about him that a woman would not like. I felt like he did not need to be reducing himself to paying for the attention or the affection from a woman. I felt terrible that I had even considered it.

He told me that I was not the type of girl that he expected either. He said, "You're wife material, and that's scary." I never took from him. Anytime he did anything for me or took me on an expensive date, it made me a little bit uncomfortable. I always worried that he thought the only reason I was spending time with him was for that. I guess I always felt ashamed I would ever meet someone like that. I was raised with conservative Christian values. Maybe what happened to me, in the end, is punishment for that.

I believed everything he told me because he never hid me. We were always out in the open. He would spend the night at my house frequently. We lived in a small town where everybody knew each other. He had answers to every question. There were times when he would ghost me. I would receive few text messages from him, but not much. I believed him when he would say he was just under a lot of pressure from work. If I pushed him too much, I would add to that, and I did not want to do that to him. I loved him. It should have been a red flag for me when he kept asking about my children and wanting to know if I would have more children. I guess those are not unusual questions for somebody to ask when considering you as a partner. He did not have any natural children of his own. He had fostered and adopted children but had no biological children. He told me very early on in the relationship that he wanted to have a biological child.

I did not realize that this man was leading multiple different lives. He had a wife of over 20 years who had grown accustomed to just looking the other way and ignoring his infidelities. He would pick up prostitutes off Backpage and Craigslist and frequent local massage parlors. He would use and abuse women that were too dumb to see through him. I did not realize any of this until it was too late. This man was so talented at deceit that he had managed to throw his wife (of over 20 years) out of their house and move my three children and me in before I had any idea.

Shortly after this happened, I had posted my kitchen table for sale online. This woman who knew me and his wife responded to the ad wanting to purchase the table. I thought it was odd that she had asked me about him and our relationship. We were not close friends or anything like that, but I chalked it up to her wanting to make conversation. She finally looked at me with that look that you know something is wrong and said, "I think you need to talk to her. I think he's playing both of you." She gave me his wife's phone number.

I contacted her and scheduled a face-to-face meeting. He had no idea, of course. When I met her, she told me everything. I was so upset. I was almost eight months pregnant. I asked her why she didn't tell me a year and a half ago. She said that she knew about me from the beginning. I can't understand why she would want to be with a man who had been cheating on her for over two decades. What kind of a woman has so little love for herself that she would allow that? Then again, who am I to judge? I had been tap dancing on the line of prostitution to feed my kids. People can call it whatever they like, and they can convince themselves that having a "sugar daddy" is a different situation, but the reality is, it's not. I never went through with actually "selling" myself, but under the context, we met, ... I guess people may view it differently. If that is the case, though, I never got my yacht. It cost me more than I could have ever imagined.

When I finally confronted him, it was a mistake. I never raised my voice. I never cursed at him. I never laid a hand on him. I would not. It was a very quiet conversation in bed. My voice is soft, so it was almost like a whisper. I said, "I know what you've been doing." I told him that I wanted him to get some therapy, and I wanted him to fire his assistant and find her another job. She was one of the many women he had been carrying on an affair with during the entirety of our relationship. She had been blowing up his phone that evening. It is easy for me to blame her (or the others) and be angry with her because she knew about me, and she knew that we were starting a family and life together. When I think about it from her perspective, she was probably just another victim of his. His targets seemed to be weak and vulnerable women. You know, single moms with little kids who secretly sit there at night and wonder if any man would look past all their baggage and love them anyway.

Women like me. When I gave him an ultimatum that he did not like, he suddenly got on top of me and started strangling me. My belly was big because I was so far along in my pregnancy. I could feel him pressing against it. When he put his hands around my neck, I remember feeling panicked. When someone strangles you, not only can you not breathe any air in, you also cannot breathe anything out. The pressure makes your face swell with blood, and it feels like it is going to pop. He was screaming at me that he was going to fucking kill me and that he was going to beat my face and black both of my eyes. I later realized that I had peed myself. He continued to put his hands on me a couple of times. All were because I had started asking questions he did not want to answer. He could sense that I knew. All of it happened so quickly.

Maybe it was two weeks; perhaps it was six weeks. I am embarrassed to admit that I have no idea. My memory of an exact timeline is not there. It is so frustrating when your mind will not work correctly because of stress. The most vicious attack was when he choked me. It was the worst one, and the last one. The weird thing is, I have these flashes of being hit, dragged, and strangled, but I cannot exactly remember in which incident that they occurred. My mind plays tricks on me when I am scared and panicked. I get flashes, not the whole thing. I remember being in the bedroom and him grabbing me by the hair and beating my head up against the wall, but I also remember being in the kitchen and doing the same thing against the thick glass window. I cannot tell you which time he hit me in the back of the head while I was sitting on the living room couch, or whether he used his fist to punch me or had a strong open hand. I do not know. I remember falling on my knees and him dragging me across the carpet by my hair, screaming at me.

I gave birth to our son alone in the hospital. I had nobody. I had to be put on IV antibiotics before and during labor for a sexually transmitted infection that I did not even know I had. I have no idea how long my womb was infected while I was carrying my baby boy. He had to see a chiropractor during his first year of life because several vertebrates in his neck were out of place. He suffered from torticollis. He could not turn his neck but to one side. Was it from the attacks? Maybe. I was told they usually see it in babies born to mothers in severe auto accidents or who suffered some significant physical trauma during late pregnancy. There is no real way to say for sure, but I believe it was likely from the attacks. It took me almost a year and a half and a lot of pressure from well-intended friends and family to be able to go out on another date.

I found it hard to be in crowds with a lot of people walking towards me at once. I was not able to go down to the boardwalk at the beach and enjoy myself because it made me so nervous about being around all those people. I had to excuse myself from meetings at work when one of my male colleagues would get loud. It did not even have to be out of anger; hearing a man yelling during a baseball game would send me into a complete panic. I could not even have a man place his hand on my arm or my shoulder for a simple pat without my back stiffening up like a board. It was a daily struggle to desensitize myself to function without it being obvious what had happened to me. It's pretty humiliating when other people can see the attack all over your facial expression or in the way you jump when a man touches you. I have always been able to appear well put together and look fine even when I was not. This time was different. It was a horrible experience, and I would not wish it on anyone.

I was naïve for overlooking all the signs. They were right there the whole time, and I just saw the good. I never let myself see his flaws. I only saw the wonderful things. You cannot let someone's good become so shiny that it blinds you from seeing the bad. I am still working on this to this day. He will show his true colors if your eyes are open to seeing them. Not everyone is good. Not everyone is terrible either. Sometimes, for whatever reason a person can be an extreme of both; good and bad. These are the most dangerous types to watch out for. As for him? He is the best and worst person I have ever met in my life. To this day, he still denies doing it. I had to make peace with an apology I never got. He still tells people that I am a liar, I am crazy, and I think some believe him. He is very convincing. Narcissists usually are from what I now read. It is not my job to convince anybody that what happened. I decided that I am not going to let him re-victimize me in any way.

Worrying about whether people believe him or me is just frustrating and hurtful. I am sharing my experience so other women going through the same thing know they are not alone. And for those who have not, keep your eyes open and protect yourself. I decided not to use his name while I was writing this. He knows his name.

You know your name, and if you are reading this, like I think you will, I want you to know I forgive you. (Not for you, but for me.)

CHAPTER TWELVE

The Foreman Girl

Andrea Foreman

As a child, I was taught, "The Foremans don't cry; they fight!" But they never told me what exactly I would be fighting. I have learned to defend myself from the world. At the age of nine, glass was shattered, and a child was no longer sleeping in her youth but falling into the hole of lost innocence.

It was every night my parents decided to take me to my aunt's. I slept in the living room by myself as my cousins slept in their bedrooms. I knew my presence would awaken him. My heart raced, hearing the creaking of his bedroom door. The pads of his feet tapping the floor lightly, trying not to wake his mother. The living room night light was flickering as I waited until his shadow pressed up against mine. His fingertips were burning against my flesh. I spread myself on the leather couch in routine. His hands were roaming to my legs, crawling into my body as if it were his own. I grew familiar with his needs, my legs moving in command to him. The covers pushed to the side, leaving me bare. It never made sense to me what exactly he was doing, but I knew in the secret of the night while the world slept, it was my job to stay still.

It was never a game, and yet I played dead for him. My eyes closed shut, breathing steady so he would not know I knew. In the comfort of his own home, he would take me over and over again with no worry of someone coming. I wondered in those moments if his heart raced just like mine when the thought of telling someone crept on me. When the sun came up, he disregarded me as if my innocence meant nothing. I was his treat at night and his secret in the morning. He hid the secret well, no longer our shadows on the walls but the ache I carried physically and emotionally. It was bearable. It had to be because the Foremans do not cry; they fight. I knew this, and yet, I was fighting my tears with the need to pull the cover from off the floor because there I was, bare to him. I was violated more by his thoughts than his hands. His greedy fingers snatched the gift of innocence.

Life was a struggle after experiencing that trauma. As if what happened was not enough, trauma hit me once again. Years later, I had experienced something that I had never gone through before. It started when my sister and I decided to smoke weed. We smoked, came in the house, and headed to the kitchen. I could not find anything to eat, so I went to sit down in the living room. I scrolled through my phone, but then a voice in my head told me to "look up." and I did. And there it was. A spirit was sitting on my brown living room couch. It was an overweight black man wearing zan orange shirt. He stuck his tongue out as if he was playing dead. I do not know how or when he got there, but I knew he was there now. Without thought, I got up quickly and sprinted into the kitchen to my sister. When I looked into her eyes, a clear thought told me, "She can't help you." So, I left the kitchen and steadily walked upstairs to my mother. As I crawled to her full of worry, a thought crossed my mind for the third time that night to wake her up gently. So, in a soft monotone, I muttered, "Mom wake up," over and over until she woke. She stared at me with a glaze over her wide eyes. With an agitated tone, she yelled, "What!" Scared and frantic, the words fell from my lips.

"I saw him. I saw him." I said with a cry hidden in my throat.

"Saw who, Andrea?"

"I saw the spirit in the living room." Fear grew in me as I said those words. Like the spirit would come and attack me for exposing him to my mother. Once I told my mom that I saw the spirit, she began praying over me. Then my sister joined, and all I could remember feeling was absolutely nothing. I did not feel scared the way I did moments ago. But then I realized I was in this weird haze. I saw things that were not there. I heard my mother and sister going in tongues, although at that moment, it did not sound like it. It felt like they were trying to attack me.

Once the haze was over, I heard my mother say, "You have to ask God to save you. Ask him for strength." So, I did. I begged him to save me, and he did. I got up and felt like me again. That was until my mother said, "Come on, we gotta get this thing out of our home." We all got our holy oil and headed downstairs. My mother began to chant a prayer that I could not comprehend. My sister began to repeat her, but I still could not grasp what she was saying, so I began to say my own. As we made it downstairs, we began to move around the living room, putting holy oil around the room. I tried to do everything my mother did, but then I saw the spirit again. This time a fire grew in me.

I felt disrespected. How dare he be in my home? I had taken my holy oil, jumped on the couch, and poured it all on where he sat. He was cocky, but my God was stronger. I was soon brought down. He attacked me, and I began to go through a haze again. I could not keep up with anything. My mind was in and out. I kept falling to the ground. I was hearing voices. Trying to keep myself together was the most challenging task when it was using my own struggles against me. That night it was revealed to me that I struggled with the spirit of laziness, lust, and arrogance.

Soon my mom and sister were praying over me again, and eventually, I came out of the pattern of hearing voices and falling to the ground. We turned some gospel on and began to praise the Lord some more. At that moment, I was still high off my adrenaline. I still was not in my right mind. I could not pinpoint what was real and fake. I was paranoid, thinking my sister was working against me. But in all, we looked to God regardless. Trying to make sense of everything, I began to sing my favorite gospel song, "Yes," by Shekinah Glory. The song reminded me of when I used to play it and cry because of how deeply I connected to it. After that night, I was no longer comfortable being alone. I hate the feeling of emptiness I feel when I am alone. It is uncomfortable and makes me anxious.

Another thing the devil stole from me was my gift of giving advice and my good communication skills. Before, whenever people came to me, I always had good feedback. I used to be a great talker, and now I am not. I was also diagnosed with schizo-affectiveness. I can say that my part in this traumatic event was that I should not have been getting high. I also should not have poured all my holy oil on the spirit.

This experience taught and revealed to me just how broken I was. Banging against the walls of her mind, knowing when he had come, she was waiting. She is my inner child, at least that is what my therapist calls her. She hides in the cracks of my beaten spirit. She flows in the pool of unresolved tears, growing comfortably in isolation, singing when someone gets too close, screaming when a guy goes too far. Fighting against myself seemed to be the most challenging of battles back then, yet I fought to succeed. He turned my thoughts into my enemies. It was easy to drown in them alone, just as he left me in those never-ending nights. But the Foremans do not cry; they fight!

In this ongoing battle, I have learned the power to say "No," not to allow myself to hide in the confinement of my mind. I have learned that I am not an object, a toy, a treat to hide at night but a woman, a body to be loved in the morning and night. To love myself was to kiss the scars and blemishes, to love myself beyond what was stolen from me. And I did. In time, I forgave him too. I forgave myself for leaving my inner child behind for so many years, and in that, we became one. I learned to love even when my heart shot with anxiety. I gained the gift of being able to cry and to fight. Life has given me more downs than ups, and because of that, I seemingly can never give up. Somehow through all the bad, I have learned to turn my battles into armor.

CHAPTER THIRTEEN

The Evening Of Torture And Tragedy

LaJuan Hawkins

I remember it so well. It started as a good evening and ended in a tragic night. It was the month of November on a Thursday evening. I was finishing my day at work from the 11 AM to 7 PM shift. I jumped in my car, and as I was driving to pick up my four-month-old daughter from the babysitter's, my mind was racing with thoughts over this unhealthy relationship between my daughter's father and me. I finally reached the babysitter's house. I walked in, and we spoke. I asked her how the baby's day went. She responded by saying that she cried a little, but her day was good overall. I packed up the baby and her belongings and walked out to the car. I sat her in the front seat and buckled her up. I began to feel very uncomfortable for some odd reason as I was leaving the babysitter's house. As I am driving and looking in my rearview mirror, I saw this person sitting in the back seat. I was frightened, and then I remembered I did not lock the doors when I got out of the car to go inside the babysitter's house. A man was sitting back there; he was my daughter's father. While I was in the babysitter's house picking up our four-month old daughter, he had gotten into the car.

All week long, we had been going through an ongoing dispute. So here I am driving home, my hands are shaking fiercely on the steering wheel as I am looking at him through my rearview mirror. I was wondering what he was going to do to me behind my head. He started to plead his case saying he was sorry for doing the things he had done and is doing in the relationship that has brought us where we are now. He was begging for me to take him back and pleading with me not to leave him. As I was driving home, the music played in the background with the lyrics "Let's Start Love Over." How ironic for that song to be playing at this moment as if it was speaking for him. As he was pleading and begging, I thought boy, this relationship is already over in my mind.

I finally made it home. I grabbed my daughter and her belongings and proceeded to walk towards the house. I turned the key and opened the door; he followed in. He came behind me and shut the door. I walked to the bedroom to put away the baby's belongings. He went into the bedroom as well. He started asking me questions one after another. He asked, "Who was it that you went out with Friday night? Was it Jerry? Where did you go?" In my mind, I thought if I answer those questions, he is going to kill me. I started to get very nervous as he paced the floor; his voice was getting louder.

By now, the baby had started to cry because of all the yelling and commotion that was going on. I still had not answered the question. I was too terrified to answer it because he told me that Jerry liked me just last week. He said he could tell by the way he looked at me when he came over to the house. He said, "If I hear that you went out with Jerry, I will kill you because that pussy belongs to me!" He expressed himself very loud and clear when saying that.

Jerry was the next-door neighbor to the right of us, who would come over from time to time and use our phone. My daughter's father would gaze at him to see if he were looking at me in some lustful way. My daughter's father was a possessive, jealous man. If anybody spoke to me, he would want to know how I knew the person. He would not allow me to go anywhere nor have company over, although he would go and come as he pleased.

So, getting back to the questions he continued to ask me, I still had not answered it yet. Finally, he said I just want to talk about it and get through it and move on towards bettering this relationship. I promise I will not be mad about it when you tell me whoever it was. He had a way of being very manipulative. I thought to myself, this man was already mad, especially since he had paced the floor. Finally, I got tired of him asking me. I just yelled out, "Yes, it was Jerry!" He walked up to me, and the next thing I saw was complete darkness and lights blinking in my head. He had punched me so hard in my left eye that I saw stars. I stumbled and fell on the floor. When I came to myself, I saw nothing but blood all over the white uniform that I had never taken off from coming in from work. I had never been hit so hard in my life. This was not the first time he hit me; he had done it several times on different occasions.

My daughter's father was a drug user, a cheater, and a beater. Now he is standing there staring at me, his mind going everywhere it could go, looking at all the blood that was on my uniform. He is gazing at me, and it has dawned on him that he is on probation, and he could go back to prison. He could be violated for violating me: how ironic. He started pacing back and forth again, saying, "I cannot go back to jail; no, no, I cannot." I stood there, face dripping in blood as my left eye began to swell. He started saying, "You need to go to the hospital, but I cannot take you because I will get arrested." I said, "Take me. I will not tell them you did this to me. I will say to them I tripped and hit my face on the corner of the table." I did not want to go to the hospital where I worked because it would be embarrassing for them to see me like this. He knew I had to go somewhere because the blood was still leaking down my face, and my uniform was now soaked with it.

He went to the kitchen and pulled out a kitchen knife from the drawer. I am wondering what he will do with that knife. He grabs me by the arm and tells me to change my clothes. He is going to take me to the hospital in Milford. He puts the knife inside of his belt in front of his pants, grabs the baby, and says, "Let's go." So, as we are walking to the car, my mind wondered if I could just get my hands on that knife, I would stab him in his chest. While opening the car door to let me in, I reached for the knife but missed it. Why did I reach for that knife and miss it? That made him even madder. He is yelling, "Why did you try to grab the knife?"

He grabbed a big ball of my hair and started dragging me as he is walking back to the house and carrying the baby as well. He shoved me back into the house, slammed the door, and threw me up against it.

The abuse started all over again. He took the knife and began stabbing me in the vagina area. He said, "You wanna fuck, don't you, huh you wanna fuck, don't you? Didn't I tell you, you belong to me? If you gave this pussy to anybody, I will kill you." He did this while the jabs in my vagina were getting harder and harder. The abuse got more intense and worse. He is steadily pressing his mouth up against my face hard and saying the same things over and over, "This pussy is mine! I will kill you; do you hear me? Do you hear me" The baby is on the couch while all of this is going on. I said, "Why don't you call the neighbor and have her come and get the baby, so she won't have to see all of this?" He called the neighbor, and she came and got her. By now, I have been in this torture for well over two hours; I was exhausted and drained from it all. "If you are going to kill me," I yelled out, "then just do it and get it over with. I am tired of you torturing me." From the knife jabs in my vagina, the hair-pulling, the punching, to the smears of his nose and mouth on my face, I did not care if I lived or died at that moment. He tells me to get my coat, and that we are going to the hospital.

Here we are on this hospital trip to Milford Memorial. He is driving like 80 to 90 miles an hour, beating and banging on the steering wheel all the while saying, "I gotta do something. I cannot go back to jail; I just cannot. I should just run us into this tree and kill us now." Now my mind is in survival mode. I thought getting back home would be safer than being on the road while he was raging. I started saying, "What about the baby? We cannot just leave her with the neighbors. What will they say or think? Why don't we just go back and get her and leave from around here? That way, nobody will know what happened, and you will not have to go back to jail. "He is terrified of going to jail, but he does not mind doing the things that could land him in jail.

We arrived back at the house, and in my mind, I am planning my getaway to safety once he goes and gets the baby from the next-door neighbor's house. Little did I know this getaway would come with a price. He tells me to go into the bedroom and take off all my clothes. Now I was frantic, all my clothes. I am thinking about what he was going to do next. I begin to take off my clothes. He is yelling, get on the bed and lay on your stomach. I am saying to myself if he tries to have sex with me, I'm just going to die right here on my own. I thought of him raping me again as he has done before in this unhealthy relationship. He grabbed my hands and put them behind my back and tied them with stockings. He then tied my feet and mouth with socks.

He walked out of the room and went out the door to get the baby from the next-door neighbors' house. I begin to think, how was I going to get out of that. There was only one way, which was to try and free myself. I started by untying the stockings from around my hands, then my mouth, and finally my feet. It was nothing but the Grace of God that allowed me to do that. I took the socks and put them on my feet. I grabbed my shirt and bra and put them on. I was terrified that he would come back and catch me. I did not put my pants or shoes on for the sake of time. I grabbed my shoes and my pants, ran out the back door, and went to my neighbors' house to the left of us. I banged so hard on the door and was yelling, "Open, please," as I kept looking back, fearing that he would see me and grab me.

The neighbor opened the door. There I stood, no pants on, just my panties and shirt and my left eye all busted up. I literally pushed him back and barged my way in, saying, "Call the cops, call the cops, please call the cops. He is going to burn my house up." My daughters' father would always say to me, "If I cannot stay in this house, nobody will. I will burn it down first." This was a brand-new mobile home that I had bought and moved in six months ago. He did not want to see me with anybody or anything if he couldn't be included in it. By now, he knew his time had finally dwindled because I had gotten away.

The neighbor called the cops for me. He was an officer that lived across the street from us. While waiting for the cops to come, I stood there peeping out of the window to see if he had come back to the house. Finally, he arrived back with our daughter. I could see his shadow moving around in the house from the reflection of the lights in the bedroom. He was peeping out of the window as well, hoping he would see me come out from somewhere.

The police arrive at the house. He came in, and I explained to them what happened. I was talking frantically, saying, "Please call for back, please, because he is gonna burn my house down if you don't." The police told me that they were not going to call for backup unless I signed a warrant against him. They said that ladies say that they want an arrest made then fail to follow through with it. So, we got into his car, and he proceeded to take me to Georgetown to Court 3 to sign a warrant. As we were riding to the court, we noticed a car traveling at a high rate of speed, flashing its lights trying to stop us. I told the cops "That's my daughter's father trying to stop us." The cops said he was not going to stop until he got to the courthouse. I told the cops to please call for backup because he would burn my house down. He still did not call for backup. We reached the courthouse, and I signed the warrant.

When we arrived back at my house, it was a shocking experience to see. There were four ambulances and three fire trucks in front of my house. My daughter's father had set my house on fire just as I said he would do. I felt a pain in my heart that I had never felt before. All that I had worked for to provide a living for my daughter and myself has gone up in smoke. I was scared because I did not know where my daughter was at the moment. I found out that he set the house on fire while she was in there with him. He had dropped her off at another friend of mine's house down the road from me, and he went on the run thereafter. That was the ending to the night of torture and tragedy for me. I did end up going to the hospital that night. It was the hospital that I worked at.

Dear LaJuan,

How are you? You should be doing awesome by now. I want you to know that you are somebody. Somebody that is beautiful inside and out. I need you to understand what you went through was not your fault. You can release yourself from all guilt, hurt, and shame. If you can look up, you can get up and move forward, never looking back at your past. The trauma that has been holding you captive, chained, and bound can no longer live there anymore. Stop letting it define who you are as a person because that is no longer who you are anymore. Set that little girl free and began to develop into that strong, powerful woman that you are. You are enough in this big bright world. Continue to walk in your own power and strength, and always remember that someone has been where you were and have blossomed as well. Keep rising; the top is never too far to be reached.

CHAPTER FOURTEEN

A Life Of Crime

Logan Wasiuta

I always thought I was a pretty girl, but at twenty-one, my confidence was slowly dwindling away when I should have been in my prime. My black, Russian, and Native-American mixed skin color was almost high yellow but a shade darker. My usual glow no longer present, with my skin looking like a foggier version of itself, almost as if something were missing from its hue. My hair was finally growing back from last summer when I had cut it extremely short into a stylish Mohawk. No more were my sides shaved, with only about two inches at the top, and it got shorter the farther back the middle went. Now my tight curls rested just below my ears and were flourishing.

I stood in the bathroom checking the time on my phone, and it read 10:26 PM. Next, I looked at my reflection in the mirror, which was something I did not usually do. Most of the time, I was too ashamed of myself to look myself in the face because I knew who I was and I was not at all who I wanted to be. I noticed that I had dark bags forming under my eyes, which was not sitting well with me. I had turned the big twenty-one three or four days prior, and all the partying I had done was starting to show on my face. Until about six months ago, I valued my appearance almost more than anything in the world. Even though I had been slacking on my self-care for the last few months, I made sure to look my absolute best on my birthday. I now had my hair hidden away with a dark brown, long flowing sew-in with a middle part, and my hair was in a loose bun at the nape of my neck.

It did not help my skin that I also had been suffering from a Percocet addiction for the past year. I wanted to quit so bad at this point that I prayed every night for God to deliver me from the prescription drugs. No matter how hard I tried to quit, I felt so physically ill that it was worse than the flu when I would not have them. So, after sniffing my nightly 10mg Percocet, I retreated downstairs in the basement to my bedroom. I was so exhausted from my day in Dewey Beach. I did not even strip out of the sweatpants and crew neck that I had put on when I got home and got out of the shower earlier.

I had started my day at 6 AM, getting up and getting cute in a teal bathing suit, jean booty shorts, and teal flip-flops. My then-boyfriend Antonio, his best friend Rodney, called Rod, and his then girlfriend Tabitha, who we called tabby, and I had all had a blast. We rode jet-ski's, swam, bar hopped, drank, and tanned the whole day. I did not return home until almost 8 PM.

Today was the last day of my birthday celebration, and I was glad it was coming to an end. My boyfriend's birthday was the 14th of July whereas mine was the 6th. We planned to just relax after the 9th until the 13th before we would begin his celebration, so we would not be too worn out. On my actual birthday, just the two of us went to Atlantic City and blew a bag in the strip club and casinos. We ended up leaving with more money than we came with. I won a lot of money on the blackjack tables.

Then the next two nights, we celebrated in my city, Dover, Delaware. We went to the casino Dover Downs that next night, and the following night we went to two little hole-in-the-wall clubs, one in Dover called Smithers that was near Wesley College, and another in Smyrna that I could not remember the name of. I knew the Smyrna club was near the Food Lion grocery store off the highway.

I was totally spent now after my day at the beach. I came home, took a shower, and my boyfriend said his other best friend called and said he needed his help with something so he would return shortly. I waved him off. I was mad that he was leaving as late as it was getting, but I could not complain because he spent the last few days with me. As soon as my head hit my pillow, I drifted off to sleep quickly.

Not soon after, though, I awoke to the sounds of my basement door opening. The door was loud when it opened from the lack of lube on its hinges, it being an old door, plus I was a light sleeper. I smiled, hearing the door open because it did not feel like I had been sleeping longer than a couple of hours. For once, my boyfriend had kept his promise and not stayed out too late.

Springing into action, I quickly threw the covers over my head and began to pretend I was sound asleep as I heard him approaching the last of the fourteen steps. Our room was sectioned off from the rest of the basement with a sheet. The other half of the basement served as a storage unit and a laundry room. I knew he would not have seen me cover-up. When the sheet was pulled back, I was not met by my boyfriend. Instead, I was met with a shiny all-black 9mm handgun. I had seen the gun a million times before with the lifestyle I lived, so I knew its exact model. Holding the 9mm was a black-masked gunman. I instantly started examining the person holding the weapon in my face. The first thing I noticed was he was a black male. He looked familiar and had a black polo hat with the purple horse and man sitting on top. He also wore a black hoodie with the white words North Face printed boldly on the left side by his heart. He had on black Levi jeans, a black book bag, and a black ski mask on his face that looked too small or too big. I could see more of his eyes and mouth than I should have been able to.

I had recognized the gunman right away after taking him in. It was my cousin Mere whose real name was Jamere. I instantly became irritated and pissed off that he and my boyfriend would pull such a seriously cruel joke. It was just like them to try and scare me, but this incident took the cake. I was ready to give them both a piece of my mind. "Stop playing! You know I know who you are, right? You and Tonio play too fucking much!" I said as I smacked the tip of the barrel of the gun out of my face. With quickness, he trained the gun back into my face with a look of pure evil. I knew my cousin, and that look well. As soon as he looked at me with his death glare, I knew he was not playing. I tried to rationalize the situation in my head because I had no beef with him, and he should not have any with me. I did not understand what the hell was going on, but I would get to the bottom of this ASAP!

Before I could say anything, he started rummaging through my room with the gun still trained on me, staying silent. That is when it dawned on me. He was here for the money! He was here for the $45,000 that I had warned my boyfriend not to tell anyone about. "Friends turn to enemies quick when money is involved." I told him the day he came home dumping out a safe full of money on our bed for me to count. I counted $46,232 cash in all sorts of different bills. He had hit a lick and hit big!

See, my boyfriend was a white and Puerto Rican mixed handsome man. He had more white privilege than he knew what to do with. Even though his family owned a blacktop business that grossed over $1,000,000,000 a year, that did not stop his hunger from being in the streets and getting illegal money. He still sold drugs, dope mainly, and robbed mutha fuckas from time to time. Plus, our Percocet addiction was expensive, so even though he made at least $1600 a week working with his family, he still lived foul. And at the place I was in my life, I was somewhat fine with it. Don't get me wrong, I wanted him to go legit and all so we wouldn't have to look over our shoulders, but I didn't want to be struggling and broke because of our addiction. I was so glad we did not have any kids.

When he tried to lift the mattress while I was still sitting on it, I snapped back into reality and became irate. "You want me to get up, dummy? How are you going to look for the money under the bed fully while I'm sitting here?" I spat angrily. This must have angered him because the next thing I knew, he snatched me up by the back of my purple crew neck without a word and started shoving me upstairs toward the level floor. When we rounded the corner from the basement to the kitchen, through the living room, into the hallway where the bedrooms and bathroom were located, I heard voices and grew nervous about what was to come. Once we approached, I saw three more men. There were two with the same type of ski mask as my cousin and one bare face with his back turned to me.

I grew nervous because everyone in the streets knew, no mask was a terrible thing. When someone wore no mask to a robbery, they usually came with intentions to kill or of much worse things such as torture and rape. What I saw next made me swallow my fear and try to save face. I let a smile creep up on my face to take the attention off whatever was going on before I got up here. All I knew was I seen my boyfriend's mother, stepfather, an aunt and step-uncle who were visiting with their 16-year-old son from Sumter, SC. His stepfather was dressed only in his tidy whitey underwear, and it broke my heart because he was the kindest old man I had ever met in my life and did not deserve this.

His cousin was sixteen but still very young-minded and did not deserve this either. Neither of the two lived a life of crime like the rest of us in the house. See, his mom, aunt, uncle, along with him and me, were all in the streets. His mom, aunt, and uncle were all under addiction as well. My boyfriend, his mom, and I did prescription opioids of all sorts, while his aunt and her boyfriend had already graduated to heroin, crack, and meth. Even though I no longer sold drugs, boosted clothes, and other various items, I did any prescription opioid I could get my hands on and still lived a life of crime in other ways.

As soon as the unmasked gunman turned around, I recognized him as well. He was a caramel complexion and had some nappy ass hair. He indeed was in dire need of a haircut. He was the only one with a white shirt, regular blue jeans, and a white t-shirt. His name was Tykee Robinson. We went to vacation bible school together every summer when we were in second grade, all the way to sixth grade. When he turned around and noticed my smile, he shouted, "Oh, this bitch thinks it's a game!" Then I felt the wind from his arm, but I was too slow to duck. He grabbed me forcefully by the left arm and smacked the left side of my head with the butt of his .40 caliber handgun that I also was familiar with.

It was shiny and silver all over, minus its wooden handle. Tears welled up in my eyes, threatening to fall, but I blinked them back, refusing to give him the satisfaction of seeing me cry. As I began to feel my face swelling, he continued, "Tell me where the money is before I blow your fucking face off!"

His mom was a crackhead growing up. Knowing how scary acting he had been and how much he got picked on because he was dirty, I highly doubted he would really shoot me, but then again, I was not sure what kind of person all the bullying and hard living had changed him into. I decided to take my chances and lie because all I had been through in life had me full of pride and turned me into a down-ass bitch who would ride or die for her man. I had too much pride to let them come in here and rob us. "I... I ...I don't know where it is." I lied, trying to look as convincing as possible. I continued…"He never tells me where he keeps his money for fear of me spending too much and making us look hot," I said, letting him know that the police would surely be on our heels if I took too many shopping sprees.

I did not want to risk anyone's life. My pride would not let these no-hustle having mutha fuckas take what my man hand risked his life and freedom for, nor was I willing to let go of the security of that much money and what it could buy. My greed was kicking in. I began an Oscar-winning performance, producing as many fake tears as I could just as I had as a child to get my way, and he did not seem fazed by it. So, I continued to try to talk my way out of the situation. "He will probably be home soon. He said he was not going to be out long. You can ask him yourself," I said, hoping he really did show up any minute, but knowing him, it would be dawn before he returned.

I knew where the money was, but I refused to tell. I would die before letting my pride go or letting my man down. I was nowhere near prepared for Tykee's next move. "I'm going to get something out of this, fuck that!" He spat, gripping me up by my arm angrily as he dragged me into the bedroom next to us. The other men keeping quiet and keeping guard on the others in the bedroom let me know Tykee ran this show. I kept hearing one of my boyfriend's best friends name, Tyreese, come from them as they started to whisper. I did not have much time to think about it with the unknown of what was to come was scaring the fuck out of me. Unsure of what was to come, I quickly became aware when I heard him unbuckling his belt buckle. I screamed, "Nooo," as I tried to make a run for it. But he quickly dragged me by my hair into the room and flung me on the bed once again, aiming the .40 caliber my way. My first thought was just to say fuck it and give the money up, but his next phrase fucked my head up.

"Even if you try to give me the money now, I'm still going to make you suck my dick with them big pretty lips and that tongue ring." With those words alone, he fucked his chances up of ever getting that money. There was no way I was going to be forced to suck his musty ass dick and give up all that damn money. He was out of his mind if he thought that I would do both! I tried my best to think of a happy place and block him out as he started to pull down my sweatpants and start his business, but it was like he wanted me to cry.

Next, he licked my face, which made me begin to wail like a child who had got their first ass whooping. I thought my sobs started to anger him the way he pressed the gun harder into my temple and began to stroke in and out of me harder and harder, but the moonlight shining in the window showed a wide grin like the cat from Alice in Wonderland. The more he pumped, the louder I wailed and the more excited he became. This drew the attention of the other men and hearing my sobs had all three of them wanting out.

Finally, I guess they could not take it anymore. Like the bad act was happening to them, they left my boyfriend's family unattended to see why I was so loud. All three of them became angry with him, saying this was not what they signed up for and told him they were out. "Y'all a bunch of bitches!" he yelled, mad that they darted out of the house. I could not believe they just took off, and no one even tried to stop him!

I guess it was true. There is no honor amongst thieves. But even still, it pained me to know one of those men were blood-related to me, and he had a daughter! Realizing they probably would not wait for him, Tykee pulled out of me and told me to open my mouth. Horrified at the thought of his semen in my mouth, I did not budge, being unwilling to open my mouth. He smacked me so hard with the gun I thought I was bleeding at first, so I just complied. Slowly opening my mouth, he began to jerk his manhood super-fast until he oozed his kids in my mouth and demanded I swallow. I faked doing so to avoid another gun blow to the head and because my dinner was threatening to creep up my throat. I heard a horn blare and could not believe they hadn't left his disgusting ass. As soon as he heard the horn, he dashed out the front door, and I was more relieved than ever before in my life.

I quickly pulled up my pants, ran to the kitchen, and grabbed the first cup I saw. It was a 2009 fake champagne flute from New Year's years ago. When spitting in that cup, I remember all I could think was the police would need some evidence to lock him away and throw away the key. After placing the cup on the counter, I lay in the middle of the living room floor and began to wail again even louder.

All my boyfriend's family members were huddled over me, rubbing my back as his mom dialed 911. Once off the phone with the officers, she called my ex, who was an hour away in Philly at a strip club. Go figure!

The following month was hell because not only did I get raped, but I lost everything. The botched robbery had put the police on our radar since my ex was already a suspect, so they raided our house. We were arrested, my ex took a plea for 18 months, and I took a gun and paraphernalia charge for my boyfriend, for which I got a year of probation. The gun charge was dropped after my probation was completed. Also, my ex had another so-called friend steal the entire amount of money from us when he trusted the guy to hold the money during our investigation.

The only good thing that came from this whole situation was I had gotten clean off the drugs, and I honestly felt like that was why God put me through another rape situation. I learned so much throughout July 2012 that I figured I would be able to make it through anything!

Because of your purchase of this book you are helping victims located throughout all three counties in the State of Delaware.

Logos CDC is donating 100% of the proceeds from the sale of this book to the Delaware Department of Justice Victims' Compensation Assistance Program (VCAP). The purpose of the DOJ Victims' Compensation Assistance Program is to alleviate some of the financial burdens faced by victims of specific offenses. VCAP provides financial assistance to help cover the costs of a variety of services that help victims and their families begin to rebuild their lives, including lost wages, medical expenses, payment for mental health counseling, and funeral expenses.

For more information about VCAP contact them directly:

DOJ Victims' Compensation Assistance Program
900 North King Street, Suite 4
Wilmington, DE 19801-3342
PH: (302) 255-1770
FX: (302) 577-1326